Phocion

THE WORLD OF PHOCION
4TH CENTURY BCE

ILLYRIA

THRACE

MACEDONIA

Abdera

Amphipolis

Chersonese
Sestus

Olynthus

Hellespont
Troy

EPIRUS

Corcyra

Crannon

THESSALY
Pherae

Aegean
Sea

Arginusae Is.
Clazomenae

Ionian
Sea

Lamia
Thermopylae

PHOCIS
Delphi
Chaeronea

BOEOTIA
Thebes
Leuctra
Plataea
Megara

Euboea
Eretria
Oropos

Chios

Clazomenae
IONIA

ATHENS

Samos

Corinth

Salamis
Aegina

PELOPONNESE

Argos
Mantinea

Megalopolis

Naxos

Sparta

Amorgos

Crete

Persian Empire

The Persian Empire extended
beyond the edge of this map, but
Phocion never visited those lands.

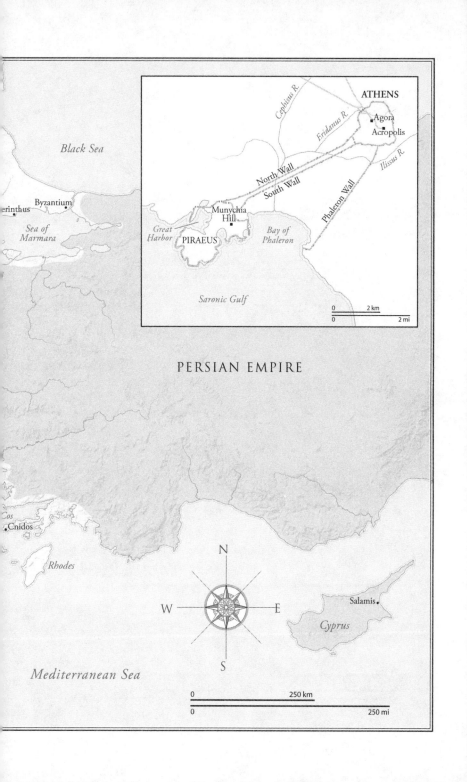

ATHENS

Agora

Acropolis

Cephisus R.

Eridanus R.

Ilissus R.

North Wall

South Wall

Phaleron Wall

Munychia Hill

Great Harbor

PIRAEUS

Bay of Phaleron

Saronic Gulf

0   2 km
0   2 mi

Black Sea

erinthus

Byzantium

Sea of Marmara

PERSIAN EMPIRE

Cos

Cnidos

Rhodes

N

W   E

S

Salamis

Cyprus

Mediterranean Sea

0   250 km
0   250 mi

Phocion

Good Citizen in a Divided Democracy

Thomas R. Martin

· ANCIENT LIVES ·

Yale

UNIVERSITY PRESS

NEW HAVEN & LONDON

Published with assistance from the foundation established in memory of
Calvin Chapin of the Class of 1788, Yale College.

Yale University Press books may be purchased in quantity for
educational, business, or promotional use. For information, please e-mail
sales.press@yale.edu (U.S. office) or sales@yaleup.co.uk (U.K. office).

Frontispiece: Beehive Mapping.

Set in the Yale typeface designed by Matthew Carter, and Louize,
designed by Matthieu Cortat, by Integrated Publishing Solutions.
Printed in the United States of America.

Library of Congress Control Number: 2024933509
ISBN 978-0-300-25663-5 (hardcover : alk. paper)

A catalogue record for this book is available from the British Library.

This paper meets the requirements of ANSI/NISO Z39.48-1992
(Permanence of Paper).

10 9 8 7 6 5 4 3 2 1

· ANCIENT LIVES ·

Ancient Lives unfolds the stories of thinkers, writers, kings, queens, conquerors, and politicians from all parts of the ancient world. Readers will come to know these figures in fully human dimensions, complete with foibles and flaws, and will see that the issues they faced—political conflicts, constraints based in gender or race, tensions between the private and public self—have changed very little over the course of millennia.

James Romm
Series Editor

To Ivy Sui-yuen Sun, who knows so well that the past is never dead

The enemies of a man are all the men who are in the household to which he belongs.

—Micah 7:6/Matthew 10:36, Septuagint Greek version/ Greek New Testament, translated by Thomas R. Martin

Contents

NOTE ON DATES   xiii

Chapter One. Phocion and the Ruin of Athenian Democracy   1

Chapter Two. Discovering a Dangerous World   13

Chapter Three. Meeting Expectations as a Teenage Boy   25

Chapter Four. Training for the Military   43

Chapter Five. Learning About Athenian Democracy   55

Chapter Six. Starting a Public Career   75

Chapter Seven. Winning Glory as a Young Naval Commander   89

Chapter Eight. Facing Midlife Challenges   103

Chapter Nine. Dealing with Macedon   117

Chapter Ten. Enduring a Catastrophe   133

Chapter Eleven. Approaching the Beginning of the End   149

Chapter Twelve. Confronting Disaster and Revenge   163

Chapter Thirteen. The Memory of Phocion, Then, Later, Now   181

Contents

CHRONOLOGY 195

SOURCE NOTES 199

NOTES 201

BIBLIOGRAPHY 205

ACKNOWLEDGMENTS 211

INDEX 213

Note on Dates

A date expressed as two numbers divided by a forward slash (e. g., 338/7) synchronizes the official Athenian calendric system with the BCE/CE calendar used today to refer to ancient history. An Athenian (solar) year began and ended in midsummer, not midwinter. Therefore, 338/7 indicates the twelve solar months from midsummer in the year today enumerated as 338 to midsummer in 337.

Phocion

CHAPTER ONE

Phocion and the Ruin
of Athenian Democracy

Phocion of Athens (ca. 402–318 BCE), officially designated a "useful and good citizen" by his home city-state, ancient Greece's most famous democracy, was elected to Athens's highest public office forty-five times, far exceeding the record of any other Athenian. But his astonishing public career of some sixty years ended in catastrophe, both for himself and for Athens. In his eighties Phocion, the longest-serving member of the board of Athenian magistrates in charge of civic and military affairs, became the designated point person to advise the government when in 322 a Macedonian would-be successor to Alexander the Great waged war against the city-state. At this precarious moment, Phocion offered policy recommendations that were not only unpopular; they contributed significantly to the ruin of Athens's treasured democracy. Defeated in battle by the Macedonians, Athens had to accept unconditional surrender to escape destruction, a humiliating failure that deprived its citizens of their cherished political freedom both at home and abroad. The Athenians blamed Phocion for their sufferings and inability to defend themselves. Angry and vengeful, they overwhelmingly condemned him to death as a traitor.

Phocion's history offers us an opportunity to ponder not only what went wrong—what led to the ruin of Athens's democracy—but how his life story might help us analyze and combat current crises afflicting contemporary democracies. This is not a new idea. As I discuss in the book's final chapter, Phocion's life and the question of how—or, indeed, whether—a democracy (from *demokratia*, "the people's power") can be a stable form of government was a prominent topic at the time of the American Revolution. Under the pseudonym "Phocion," Alexander Hamilton wrote political manifestos in which he argued that a democracy that gave voters unlimited power to make all decisions by majority vote, as in Phocion's Athens, was destined to end in disaster. Hamilton interpreted Phocion's biography as evidence that ruin would ensue in a political system whose decisions on every political and legal issue were determined by the majority composed of, to use ancient Greek terminology, "the many" (*hoi polloi*): that is, people who, though citizens, were not members of the social elite. By choosing to write as "Phocion," Hamilton was seeking to marshal support for his preconceived view that the nascent United States should not be governed indiscriminately by voters who had neither social standing nor constitutional restraints.

In light of today's fiercely combative political disputes about the best way to structure governments, it again seems worthwhile to examine Phocion's long public career and ultimate fate. To do so we must return to the ancient sources for his life (discussed in the Source Notes). The overwhelming majority of our surviving information comes from the renowned ancient Greek author Plutarch (ca. 50–120 CE), a biographer and philosopher who also served as priest of the god Apollo at his oracular shrine in Delphi. Plutarch's *Parallel*

Lives, a collection of biographies pairing a famous Greek leader with a famous Roman leader, became extremely popular in the early modern period and remains so to this day.

Plutarch's paired lives examine the character, successes, and failures of his biographical subjects as examples for his readers of how to live their own lives. Extremely well read in the earlier ancient authors whose works provided information about the history of Phocion's time and life, Plutarch pairs Phocion's biography with that of Marcus Porcius Cato of Utica, a controversial figure in Rome's history in the first century BCE. Cato became embroiled in the internal political struggles of his homeland and, like Phocion, came to a catastrophic end, killing himself as the Roman Republic self-destructed when Julius Caesar and his enemies violently competed for power.

Plutarch's Life of Phocion, written some six hundred years after its subject's death, characteristically pays considerably less attention to the historical events of Phocion's life than to his character and personal behavior. And Plutarch's lack of discussion concerning events at Athens in Phocion's lifetime is unfortunately not offset by other surviving ancient sources. Consequently, there are significant periods of Phocion's life when the best that can be done in a modern biography is to provide contextual information on the situations in question without supplying specific details about Phocion's own actions. To study Phocion, we have to focus on the circumstances of his life and times, how he was likely to react to them psychologically, and what he was likely to do in response.

Key to any understanding of Phocion is the recognition that in his time Athenians were expected to conduct themselves in accordance with an unshakeable sense of *belonging* to their society, a society that was extremely proud of its ancestral history. As modern psychological research, especially on social identity theory, has repeatedly demonstrated, a sense of belonging is one of the strongest emotions motivating both unity within a community and conflict with other communities. It is essential to the successful functioning of a democracy.

Born into a well-off family, Phocion gradually learned what it meant to be a boy and to be free rather than a girl or a slave in Athenian democracy. With his family's help in his first two decades of life, he successfully passed his city-state's tests of legitimacy and navigated its strenuous rites of passage. This extended process officially guaranteed his status as one who belonged in the strictly regulated society of participating (male) citizens in Athens's democracy. As an adult, Phocion showed himself never hesitant to criticize the unnamed "many" whose majority vote determined Athens's domestic and foreign policies. But he also regularly and strongly rebuked members of the political elite whom he saw as threatening the city-state's safety.

Related questions therefore need to be addressed in this narrative. First is the issue of Phocion's reaction to conventional expectations of how a male citizen should publicly demonstrate his allegiance to the communal identity treasured by his contemporaries. Second, and crucially, what were the likely consequences for Phocion of his characteristically confrontational comments to other citizens after they evidently came to regard him as having no genuine sense of "belonging" with them?

In his study of Phocion's character, Plutarch devotes a great deal of attention to his subject's rhetoric. He especially emphasizes Phocion's tendency to direct harshly phrased public statements at his fellow citizens, criticizing their political decisions, especially when the stakes were high for the communal safety of the Athenians. Plutarch's Life of Phocion, in fact, includes more than sixty quotations of strongly worded comments that Phocion made in public life. Not a single one is positive in its evaluation of his fellow citizens. The use of pointed, even insulting language in criticism of others was frequent in ancient Athenian society and politics, but Phocion stands out for the consistent harshness of his remarks. In his public life, he frequently presented himself as a vocally aggressive and blunt curmudgeon. He often spoke disparagingly about other Athenian citizens, especially those who were not rich enough to be considered members of the upper class. At the same time, however, he always served with distinction in the armed forces during the Athenians' decades-long struggles with other Greeks and foreign powers throughout the fourth century BCE.

Strikingly, Phocion also openly shunned the accepted norms of male social life in the relatively small elite stratum of citizens into which he had been born. As we will see below, he refused to join in the evening drinking parties that his male peers frequently organized to discuss political and social questions, functions that strengthened their bonds as self-proclaimed movers and shakers at Athens. On the other hand, whenever he had official dealings with non-Athenians, he seemed to get along more cordially with these strangers than with his own countrymen. It is therefore hard to pinpoint instances of Phocion's making much effort to express that valued sense of belonging with other Athenians — of any social class.

It is clear that Phocion always remained openly loyal to his homeland and devoted himself to what he saw as the necessary policies to keep it safe. He also behaved with scrupulous integrity, more than once rejecting a huge bribe offered to influence his political stance. At the same time, his denigration of his fellow citizens was especially frequent and biting when he saw them falling short in supporting what he regarded as the definition of Athens's national interest: preserving its safety above all other considerations, including its citizens' fierce pride. During his lifetime, as Athens's previously unrivaled dominance as the major power in the central Mediterranean world gradually weakened, Phocion unswervingly advocated what he saw as the policies most likely to preserve the *soteria* of Athens as a community. This ancient Greek notion literally means salvation — that is, *being* saved, not just by one's own actions but with the assistance of others. Phocion accepted the idea that the Athenians' communal soteria involved relying not solely on their own efforts but, when necessary, on those of other people — and always on the goodwill of the gods.

In this context, in evaluating the controversial policy recommendations late in his career that called for Athens to accept uncomfortable compromises with aggressive foreign powers, we must foreground Phocion's preoccupation, which was almost an obsession, with safety. On such occasions, his advice could provoke red-hot opposition from many other Athenians, but he never relented. To paraphrase an observation from Plutarch about the best approach for those who wanted to be politically influential in a Greek city-state, "Being appealing and inspiring is even better than being as rich as Croesus!" Phocion clearly rejected this point of view.[1]

Phocion's resolute bluntness about politics was certainly principled. When advising his fellow citizens to come to terms with foreign potentates whom they much preferred to resist, it was never because he had secretly accepted money from these rich outsiders to back their plans. In addition, he never abused his office or stole public funds, unlike some other Athenian political leaders. When financial hardship struck him in midlife, instead of resorting to political corruption, he accepted a dangerous command as a mercenary fighting outside his homeland to restore his prosperity. In his private life, he showed generosity even to people to whom he was not close but who desperately needed help financially.

Phocion first made a name for himself in Athenian society in

The Ruin of Athenian Democracy

his twenties through his military service. By his mid-forties, he had also achieved prominence as a political leader. He was active during the Athenians' struggles beginning in the mid-fourth century to preserve their traditional independence in the face of threats posed by the aggressive new power exerted in Greece by the kingdom of Macedon. First Philip II and then his son and successor Alexander III (Alexander the Great) took aggressive action to dominate the Greeks. The Athenians' efforts to stop these kings did not succeed, militarily or politically. Matters grew much worse for the Athenians during the turmoil that erupted throughout Greece in the years following Alexander's premature death. Phocion ended up being denounced by nearly all his fellow citizens as the poison (*pharmakos*) principally responsible for Athens's catastrophic downfall in this tumultuous period. After the majority of Athenians had voted to put him to death, they demonstrated the extremity of their anger by having his remains cast out over their border. The citizens among whom Phocion had once belonged now literally removed him from their membership.

Deepening the mystery of Phocion's shocking fate is that the Athenian citizens chose to dishonor a man who, despite his notable shortcomings in sociability, they had at one point officially lauded with the honorific title of *Chrestos*. This multivalent term designated a citizen who had proved himself especially "useful and good" to the community. The honor was perhaps conferred on Phocion as official recognition of his financial support for Athenians who had suffered family tragedies. Or it might have been due to his successes as a commander in battle. Whatever the immediate reason for the honor, Phocion's overall behavior as a citizen clearly reflects his unwavering dedication to making himself chrestos to his community. He always tried to steer Athens on what he saw as the best course to keep it safe during increasingly perilous times. As he once sharply said to fellow citizens abusing him for his cautious policy as a general at a time of great danger, "Oh you blessed ones, choose safety first!"[2]

In the later years of Phocion's life, the Athenians had to confront the growing chasm between their memory of Athens's former supremacy among Greek states and its present severely reduced international power. Where before they had lived in an independent democracy, they now had to mold their policies to fit the demands of the unexpectedly powerful monarchs to their north. As one of Phocion's contemporaries in Athenian public life lamented, Athens's ship of state had suffered "a shipwreck." The Athenians' emotional dismay at their severe loss of autonomy dramatically heightened the political discords raging among them over both domestic and international politics.[3]

Unfortunately for Phocion — and for Athens — his judgment as a political leader fell short of the demands of the events overtaking the city-state during the fateful final years of his life. Overall, he seems to have miscalculated what was best for Athens in an era of increasingly acrimonious political divisions, advocating policies of accommodation with the Macedonians that put him too far out of sync with the majority of Athenians. Worst of all, as it would turn out, in the period after Alexander's death Phocion seriously misjudged the trustworthiness of the foreign commanders with whom he sought to negotiate for Athens's safety, perhaps because he regarded them as fellow members of the social elite and therefore honest and reliable.

In the end, his fellow citizens labeled him a traitor specifically as the result of one indisputably catastrophic decision made at a crucial moment during the series of violent crises engulfing Athens. But as we will see, Phocion had himself paved the way for his fall from political grace through his habit of adopting a harsh and self-righteous critical tone in his public speaking. This behavior finally pushed his countrymen to condemn him as a result of his seemingly constant denial of his belonging among them.

Phocion turned out to be mistaken in his belief that the Athenians on the whole would continue to see him as genuinely wanting to be useful and good to them even when he regularly berated them for their perceived misperceptions and misjudgments of crucial situations. Disastrously, he failed to understand that being a good citizen in the sense of being a useful citizen meant being other-directed. In short, he was unable to figure out how to care about his community as a whole while also dealing effectively with the majority of the individuals who comprised it. Behaving much like a father angry at the uncooperative children who defied commands meant to ensure their safety, he failed to convince the majority of his fellow citizens that he truly was useful and good because he was apparently attached to the *idea* of a city-state as a community but was not able to accept emotionally the *social and psychological reality* of belonging to it.

Soon after Phocion's ignominious public execution in 318, an authoritarian government took over Athens. Its autocratic leader ordered that Phocion be commemorated as a heroic defender of the city-state who had been wronged by an ignorant and heartless mob. And as I mentioned briefly above, two millennia later the story of how to interpret Phocion's life acquired yet another startling dimension: in early modern times he was hailed as a heroic defender of a "proper" government combating mob rule, an example to be followed in contemporary life. In seventeenth- and eighteenth-century France as in Revolutionary-era America, Phocion was resurrected as a beacon of integrity and insight by intellectuals, politicians, and artists. By heroizing Phocion, these early-modern commentators were condemning what they regarded as a prime example of the political disorder and injustice they associated with "the many." For them, the fate of Phocion became a proof of the alleged flaws of unrestricted democracy.

Any biography (from the Greek for "the writing of a life") must by the nature of the genre be selective, even when it is an autobiography. No one, not even the biographical subject, can possibly report all the emotions, actions, and luck both good and bad that ultimately define the course of a human life and career. This truism is especially valid for the life of Phocion because, to repeat a salient fact about his biography, the surviving ancient sources fail to report many, many details from his history. Furthermore, in this biography I do not claim to present a comprehensive interpretation of Phocion meant to rebut other opinions of him. Modern scholars of ancient Greek history disagree strongly in their overall assessments of Phocion. Evaluations of Phocion range from a capable leader who did his best for his homeland during an extremely difficult period but also made crucial mistakes, to a political nonentity. In the latter view, Phocion's reputation as a philosophical hero treated cruelly by the ignorant crowd was puffed up after his death, first in Athens by an autocrat and then much later in Europe by democracy-hating elitists.

I wrote this book with overlapping goals. In the first place, I hoped to show why the biography of Phocion is worth reading for its own sake as an evocative tale of the tragedy of a well-meaning but flawed protagonist. But I also meant it as a stimulus to readers to identify issues and quandaries that will be "good to think with" concerning our own times, when democracy seems to be threatened throughout our world. The concept of "good to think with" (to use its often-repeated English translation) reflects a crucial insight by the French anthropologist Claude Lévi-Strauss in his study of totemism: we can benefit ourselves by reflecting on the thoughts and behaviors of peoples in cultures different from our own. The Athenians' catastrophic failure to resolve their differences during the last decades of Phocion's life effectively condemned their city-state to never-ending uncertainty, a condition of flux that helped fuel its decline. The inability of Athenians to unite eventually culminated in the suppression of Greece's most famous democracy.[4]

Ancient Greeks evaluated public figures above all on how these men (and in the patriarchal world of Phocion, all formal political leaders were men) acted and spoke in service of "the shared advantage and benefit" (*koinon sympheron,* as the ancient Greeks termed the common good). Especially when a community was under severe pressure, those evaluations could differ dramatically, because then as now no agreement existed on what in fact constituted shared advantage and benefit, the useful and good that should belong to all in common. The continuing lack of agreement today on such a critical topic in social and political policy therefore seems a compelling reason to analyze Phocion's biography as best we can. As I write this book in the United States in 2023, political rhetoric is fiercely inflamed, violent protests are occurring, and secession from the federal union is even on the table in some quarters.

Phocion's story seems once again to resonate strongly. It points to an unsettling quandary for democracy in the current political environment: the need to find a productive way forward for individuals and for their communities when citizens' disagreements become so polarized and bitter concerning how to promote the shared advantage and benefit that these disputes threaten to destroy the polity. Without doubt we need to try to mitigate the destructive emotional effect of so much aggressive speech and action and create at least a hope for mutual cooperation going forward. The Athenians of Phocion's time failed to do this. We today need to do better.

This biography of Phocion will more closely resemble a mosaic with many missing pieces than a fully delineated portrait. Nevertheless, it can also be relevant to arguments raging today about which approach to government best supports our shared advantage and benefit in a perilous world. In short, it seems both useful and good to ask what we can take away from the story of Phocion that will be good to think with about the future of our democracy and about how we as citizens and leaders can promote everyone's shared advantage and benefit. Phocion's ancient life merits consideration in this context because, as William Faulkner wrote in *Requiem for a Nun,* "The past is never dead. It's not even past."

CHAPTER TWO

Discovering a Dangerous World

The ancient sources on Phocion report nothing specific about his early years, not even the exact date of his birth near the end of the fifth century BCE. Nevertheless, our knowledge of ancient Greek life in general provides insights about the kind of childhood he would have experienced, and this in turn reveals probable influences on his personal and psychological development. Particularly important for his later life would have been the process of coming to realize that the underlying reality of his world was often not what it had originally seemed to him.

Greeks of Phocion's time recognized that childhood experiences deeply affect people's future approach to their lives, emotionally, cognitively, and physically. Plato's observation that the things children learn have an amazing staying power in their memories summed up a familiar saying. Human beings obviously develop in widely diverse ways based on their genetic inheritance and socioeconomic circumstances. So not every boy in ancient Athens would have reacted in the same way to the conditions of childhood described here. Some clearly reached different conclusions from Phocion's about how to conduct themselves in response to their gradual discovery of the confusing aspects of their society. Some of them, if their resources permitted, clearly decided that the only viable option under such conditions was a relentlessly dissolute and self-indulgent existence. But hedonism in any form manifestly did not become Phocion's choice for his future course.[1]

All that we know about Phocion's father is his name, Phocus. For his mother, we lack even that most basic fact. We cannot determine whether she came from a family wealthy enough to bring a substantial dowry to her marriage, as was expected of brides from financially secure families. If she did, that capital, according to Athenian law, formally remained her — or rather her original guardian's — property. Women in Athens were always, legally, under the guardianship of a close male relative. At her death, it passed to her children in support of their prospects as future parents themselves.

In ancient Athens, as in every other human society, money made a huge difference to an individual's trajectory in life. Ancient authors diverge on the financial standing of Phocion's family. According to Plutarch, the near-contemporary Greek biographer and politician Idomeneus (ca. 325–ca. 270 BCE) insisted that Phocion must have come from an undistinguished family because his father was a manual laborer who made pestles. The first century BCE Roman historian Cornelius Nepos in *his* brief biography baldly states that Phocion was always poor. Plutarch, however, emphatically contradicts assertions that Phocion came from a family that had fallen from its place in the world. The Greek biographer confidently concludes that Phocion came from an affluent, upper-class family, and he bases this assessment on the known fact that Phocion attended Plato's Academy for his higher education. This was a private association that only the wealthy could attend because they did not have to spend their days working to support themselves and their families.[2]

Evidence from Phocion's adult career reveals that he did, in fact, possess substantial property and liquid capital. Otherwise, he could not have served as the commander of a naval warship, a post that required a high level of expenditure from the commander's private funds. Phocion held this position when he was still only in his mid-twenties. Since he would not have been able to make a sufficient fortune on his own by that age, he must have inherited the property that made this costly public service possible. This private fortune probably went back at least two generations in his family: another Phocion also had served as a naval commander in a famous sea battle between the fleets of Athens and Sparta about nine years before Phocion's birth. Since the name "Phocion" was rarely found in ancient Athens, this man was surely his grandfather.

Phocion's family's prosperity set him apart from the great majority of his contemporaries, whose lower economic status compared to that of the social elite led the latter to dismiss "the many" as "the poor." This condescending label applied even if "the poor" earned enough to keep their families fed, clothed, and housed. Of course, being rich at Athens made life easier than being poor in manifold ways, especially because being poor meant having to work hard just to make a living. Still, Phocion's experiences during his earliest years in a financially secure family that owned slaves would have produced lasting effects on his later life and personality.

As a young child, for example, Phocion would never have been left hungry or alone. All the same, he eventually came to understand that he and everyone else existed in a world that was always and forever full of danger. Safety was supremely important but frighteningly elusive, starting at birth. Babies in Phocion's day died with distressing frequency. Many did not survive birth or the early weeks and months of their lives. Problems during birth, infections, accidents, and, for some, desperate poverty guaranteed a seemingly never-ending supply of infant corpses, a reality that the young Phocion could not have avoided.

In addition, over time Phocion would have discovered that babies might be abandoned, even by families like his who could afford to raise them. Exposure, a drastic but accepted procedure, was one option when a family — almost always the father — decided that the baby was not worth raising. Reasons for exposure could range from the infant being regarded as somehow physically less than perfect to the suspicion that it was the product of an illicit love affair by its mother. Such neonates would be left alone somewhere outdoors, often at a location known to be a drop-off spot for unwanted babies. There they might die; conversely, anyone passing by could find them and take them away. They would then either be reared as members of the family or sold into slavery for a profit. Protected children who eventually came to realize that they had been fortunate enough to have escaped this devastating fate could have reached only one conclusion: uncertainty — indeed life-threatening uncertainty — was a constant of the human condition.

The ongoing risk to life hardly diminished as children grew older. Overall, from a quarter to half the children born in Phocion's time did not survive to adulthood. Diseases or fatal accidents would have taken away more than one childhood friend of Phocion's. And when a mother went into labor with another baby, it was not just the baby that was at risk. The living children might also soon find themselves bereft of a mother. Women died so often in childbirth that the peril achieved legendary status. As a grownup, Phocion would be able to fully appreciate a famous line from a play by the fifth-century BCE Athenian tragedian Euripides, in which the formidable (foreign) protagonist Medea brusquely compares a woman giving birth to a man in wartime combat. She proclaims, "I would rather fight in an infantry battle three times than give birth only once!" It seems likely that many Greek women agreed with her.[3]

A large percentage of children experienced the loss of a mother or father; the latter were always at risk of dying in one of Greece's frequent wars, as well as of falling prey to disease or accident. Athenian children with both parents still alive were accordingly recognized publicly as special because, as Plato expressed their situation, they were regarded as "flourishing on both sides." To signal their fortunate status, they were singled out to make special appearances at religious festivals and weddings. This custom expressed the hope that their good luck would somehow spread to other youngsters. Phocion might have experienced this celebrity status; we are not told whether his parents died early. But we have no irrefutable information about how long his parents lived, so Phocion may have been excluded from official recognition as a member of the privileged group of flourishing children. In that case, seeing other children who still had both parents at their sides being paraded in public as special would have been a persistent memory and further emphasized how precarious was the safety that human beings crave. Based on his later insistence as a political leader on safety first in public policy, it seems likely that he absorbed this lesson in depth.[4]

There were many more enduring truths for him to discover as a young boy living in fourth-century Athens. Even if a child survived the hazards that attended birth in a society lacking hospitals and emergency medical services, countless other dangers still loomed in daily life, both in the crowded environment of urban Athens and in the scores of smaller country settlements scattered throughout the surrounding territory. When the young Phocion walked through his community, he encountered numerous families who constituted the significant percentage of Athenians who were impoverished by any standard, ancient or modern. Himself well fed, he discovered that lack of food was always a threat for many other children, regardless of whether their older family members made a living as day laborers in the main city or as subsistence-level farmers and hired workers in the countryside. He was extremely fortunate to belong to the social stratum that had inherited money, owned income-producing agricultural land, or made a good living from workshops manufacturing items for sale.

But not even relatively well-off children such as Phocion had access to specialized therapies to help them recover from injuries. Accidental falls or contusions from corporal punishment that caused internal bleeding could prove fatal because there was no effective surgery to repair the damage. Even more widespread was the danger of infection. No effective medical treatments existed to lessen the suffering and mortality these ailments caused. Bacterial illness, in particular, could strike at any time, spread by sources ranging from polluted water to unsanitary conditions created by the lack of hygienic toilet facilities. As Phocion would have found out once he was old enough to understand the sanitation system used in most well-off Athenian households, human excrement was collected in containers in the house and then disposed of outside. The urban center had sewage channels for this human waste and stormwater, but there was no way to disinfect the contents. Since there were no local health facilities to house the sick and dying, the afflicted remained at home in view of their family's children. Finally, Phocion, like other children and adults, had to endure frequent close contact with dead bodies that had been left in Athens's narrow streets by those too poor to dispose of them. Municipal workers periodically came around to gather up these foul-smelling remains for disposal.

Phocion inevitably would have had firsthand experience of the emotional consequences of having people close to him die, perhaps even at home before his eyes. Like other young people, he would also have participated in funerals, accompanying the dead bodies to the gravesite and later revisiting the cemetery with other members of the family to pay homage to lost family members. In short, Phocion, like every ancient Greek child, grew up deeply aware of the likelihood of encountering serious misfortunes in life, up to and including death. His earliest years taught him this lesson, which sometimes escapes children today who are fortunate enough to grow up in the far safer, far less fraught environments of prosperous and peaceful communities.

Losing children to disease or accident or violence was so prevalent in ancient Greece that adoption of adults, especially men, was a common practice. In the patriarchal society of ancient Greece, the hope was that these adoptees would produce surviving male children of their own, thereby continuing the line of descent of the adopting family. As the probably non-Athenian speechwriter Isaeus (ca. 420–340s BCE) once remarked concerning an inheritance case, adoption provided "the only escape from desolation and psychological consolation for childless human beings." No adoptions are attested in Phocion's family, but he would eventually have come to realize their ubiquity in his world.[5]

Phocion, then, must have discovered the reality of pain and death firsthand and up close while still a child. He had to have become keenly aware of the fragile mortality of human beings. No one was spared. The women who bore the children to keep human society going were risking their lives, and so were the men who devoted themselves to military and public service. Phocion's inevitable awareness of this melancholy truth was likely a strong motivation for his insistence as an adult that Athenians must minimize their risk when conducting international relations in a world that had dramatically changed in ways dangerously not to their advantage. Regardless of his fellow citizens' wishes, he consistently instructed them to accept unwelcome compromises for the sake of safety. It seems plausible to think that he maintained his political policy of "safety first always" at least in part because he had been so deeply and permanently affected emotionally by his childhood introduction to the omnipresent dangers of life.

Childhood also taught Phocion that surface appearances could be deceptive and that there was a lot to be discovered about the realities lurking underneath them. Young children, both girls and boys, lucky enough to survive birth and be raised in a family with good financial resources lived their first years primarily in the company of women. So at the start of his life Phocion would have been looked after by his mother (probably), female relatives, and women slaves. Ancient Greece was a slave-holding society, and well-off families kept enslaved domestics to help with childrearing, including wet nursing. In families that had permanent houses, a section of the dwelling would be set aside as the women's area: nonfamily older males would ordinarily not enter those rooms. Phocion would have spent his first years predominantly in this female company. In this special space, Phocion as he first interacted with the world would have been with women whose specific legal status would have been unclear to him. All he would know was that they fed, cleaned, clothed, and paid attention to him.

So at first Phocion would have had no notion of the difference in the freedom and social status accorded to, say, his mother as a free person and the other women who nursed and groomed him in their roles as wet nurses and household slaves. Just looking at them would give him no good clues about their status. Gradually, however, he would have discovered that the people who took care of him could be quite different from him, not just in their gender but also in their personal autonomy. For him as a child gradually becoming more aware of his world, it must have been baffling to try to grasp why these people who looked like him and took care of him were themselves radically differentiated from him in their power to control their own lives. They fed him when he was hungry, coddled him when he was scared, played with him, helped him go to sleep, and much more.

To put it another way relevant to Phocion's case, these unfree women were useful and good to him. As surviving documents reveal, even enslaved persons could be praised with the same powerful term that Phocion himself later earned as a public acclamation for his public virtue. Yet Phocion would eventually learn that these useful and good people close to him could also at any time be taken away forever. They could be sold, beaten physically, sexually assaulted, even killed with impunity. What kind of world was this? he would have wondered. People who on the surface looked like him and looked after him could have such horribly divergent states of being for their underlying reality. Death, he thereby would come to understand, was not the only hidden menace hiding in the baffling darkness of human fate. The absence of freedom that could hide under surface appearances also threatened people's safety.

Like his contemporaries growing up in comfortable households, Phocion would have had to puzzle over how to distinguish who was who, who was higher ranking and who was subordinate, whom to trust and whom to reject. As an older child, he would have come to know that resolving the ambiguities governing the autonomy of those close to him mattered a great deal. The realities of their conditions determined how he should behave toward them according to contemporary social conventions. In other words, Phocion would have become aware that the concept of belonging to a community was far from simple. "Belonging" and "community" could not easily be determined except thorough careful investigation. In these ways, his early experiences would slowly teach him that it was perplexing but crucially important to try to determine the ultimate reality of things rather than rely on superficial assumptions. This concern was paramount, he would learn, to the crucial and enduring issue of the relationship between identity and safety.

By Phocion's later youth, he would have come to realize how fortunate he had been to escape the loss of autonomy plaguing the lives of the many Greek youngsters who were enslaved, or free but indisputably poor. Once these children were old enough to follow instructions and work reliably — probably around seven years old — their daily lives required near-constant physical labor either to serve their owners as slaves or, as free youngsters, to help their families secure a basic living. Since in common with the rest of the Greek world except Sparta, Athens provided no free public education, the children of poor families had scant chances to learn reading and writing even at an elementary level. Many never succeeded in achieving literacy and therefore depended on oral communication to gain information and form opinions, not least concerning their positions on political policies. Gossip in the streets about what Athens's leaders were thinking and planning powerfully influenced the formation of many people's political leanings.

Phocion's young life as a member of the social elite at Athens would have been very different from that of the city-state's poorer residents. As a male child, once he reached the age of seven, he would have begun his formal — that is, private and paid — education. Athens provided no public funding to subsidize private education, except for boys whose fathers had been killed fighting in the citizen militia. This was Athens's main land-based military force until, later in Phocion's lifetime, it became more common to hire mercenaries to supplement or substitute for armed citizens. Most Athenian male citizens fought as sailors in the navy (discussed below). The families of fatherless boys received a stipend that could be spent to hire a free teacher or buy an enslaved one. Girls received their instruction at home from older relatives or from trusted, literate household slaves. Poorer families did what they could to educate their children at home or through work experience assisting family members.

Boys at this age whose fathers were still alive began to spend more time in the company of males. This change in their daily environment usually brought stricter discipline. We lack any evidence for Phocion's relationship with his father. Indeed, we do not even know whether his father lived long enough to be a major figure in Phocion's life after he emerged from the more accommodating atmosphere of the women's quarters. For all we know, Phocion's father may have died early in his son's life. In any case, Phocion's relatives would have had to figure out how to arrange for the family children to acquire the level of training in literacy and other skills that their socioeconomic status made possible. They then would have had to pay for this private education. For boys such as Phocion, families with sufficient resources usually assigned a special slave to oversee boys' daily lives. These pedagogues (from the Greek for "those who lead a child") were men. Their main tasks were to shepherd the boys around and keep them from trouble when out of the house.

If a pedagogue was literate and numerate and could be trusted not to abuse the boy sexually, he could also help his young charge start to learn his letters and numbers, while focusing on a pedagogue's primary duty to guide the child in developing socially acceptable manners and motivations. This was almost certainly the case with Phocion. Then, beginning when the boy was between seven and ten years old, his slave teacher would have accompanied him to a private school. There professional teachers, themselves free men, charged tuition to provide the elementary education appropriate to Phocion's social standing. As Phocion began to approach adolescence, these small classes in the company of the sons of other well-off families would gradually have moved on to more detailed study of literature, history, philosophy, and music.

The understanding Phocion gained about life during his childhood would have mattered when he later embarked on his adult career. Of particular importance was what he learned about the complicated task of forming an accurate perception of critical situations. His understanding of how interstate relations affected the independence of communities like Athens guided his decisions throughout his entire career. Were his contemporaries right, he often had to ask himself, to think it slavery for them to accept political compromises demanded by super-powerful foreigners? Making such a choice could hardly be trading freedom for enslavement when it was the only path for safety, he must have concluded. Such a policy would have seemed to him a liberation, at least of a sort, rather than an enslavement. As will become clear later, the longer Phocion lived, the more pressing this dilemma became for him politically as an adviser to and leader of his fellow citizens. In the end, his misjudgment of a key person in just such a context decided his own fate.

CHAPTER THREE

Meeting Expectations as a Teenage Boy

Teenage boys in Athens who were well off enough not to have to work every day to help support their families participated in a variety of activities that readied them to take on the responsibilities and attitudes of a publicly active adult male citizen. Vigorous physical training represented an essential component of this preparation. Devotion to fitness was meant to remain a constant feature of their lives until injuries or advanced age rendered them incapable of action in war or competitive sports. Athens had facilities both private and public devoted to this goal, gymnasiums ("places to be naked"), as they were known.

The emphasis on developing physical fitness and strength reflected both universal Greek standards of male beauty and, in particular, Athenian democracy's military policy. To defend the homeland against attacks or pursue expansionist foreign expeditions, Athens needed to be able to field as many men as possible. These men had to be prepared for demanding service in the citizen militia and develop a keen desire to win. Their civic responsibility called for Athenian men to have the muscles and the endurance to fight in diverse roles. As heavy infantry, they carried weapons and armor whose weight might exceed half that of their own bodies. As armored cavalrymen, they charged at speed to scatter massed opponents. As rowers on warships, they wielded long oars to propel their ram-equipped hulls into collisions meant to disable enemy vessels. I shall enlarge upon the nature and consequences of these military expectations below, in my discussion of Phocion's early adult life.

The athletic training required for a desirable male image and military fitness always involved competition. Indeed, competition informed almost every aspect of ancient Greek life, from the production of plays in the city's large theater to the dynamics of love, especially between males. As part of his near-constant physical training in his teens, Phocion would be expected to compete in sports such as running and throwing and martial arts. Once he reached the age of fourteen, one-on-one contests for his age group greatly increased in intensity. These competitions included a brutal wrestling-cum-boxing match called the *pankration* (every strength) that could leave participants with serious injuries. Quitting the arena of male rivalry was not an option for any upper-class Athenian youth who had eyes on his public reputation and future influence in Athens's direct democracy. Phocion therefore would have had to take his lumps like his other contemporaries.

At this stage of his development Phocion would have experienced regular corporal punishment at the hands of his teachers, trainers, and male relatives. He could expect blows when he failed to meet their expectations – or, indeed, if the supervising adults simply felt like demonstrating their superiority. Athenian boys seem to have escaped the fierce public whippings meted out to Spartan youths who failed to participate energetically in a public competition that required them to steal from an altar of the gods and then escape uncaptured. Still, the emphasis in Athens, and in every other ancient Greek community, remained on victory, not simply the thrill of competing. Winners would bask in the praises of their elders, while losers would be mocked. The adult Phocion's tendency to infuse his public comments with a bullying tone perhaps had some roots in this unpleasantly unforgettable early experience.

Sexual contact with an older male was another aspect of adolescent life for many Athenian boys. This experience was common to those who spent time working out in a gymnasium under the gaze of the adult men who exercised there. There were laws and customs meant to regulate the nature of an erotic relationship between a young man, designated the beloved, and the older one who pursued him, called the lover. These regulations were intended to protect the well-being of the beloved and his future prospects of becoming a respected citizen, but enforcement was problematic. Greek city-states had varying regulations in this regard — in particular concerning the acceptability of intercourse.

In Athens an erotic relationship between an older man and an adolescent was not illegal. It was, however, the convention that whatever happened emotionally and sexually between the pair, the relationship was supposed to support social maturation and character formation for the beloved and not simply crude carnal satisfaction for the lover. Moreover, a spirit of competition was meant to infuse the relationship. The beloved was expected to resist attempts by a lover to dominate him, while the lover saw himself as driven to achieve his goals. Social norms called for the aspirations of a lover to be to mold his younger charge in accepted modes of adult male social behavior, but in reality a lover could be aiming merely to satisfy the physical desire he felt for his beloved.

Such pairings were expected to dissolve once the beloved became a full-fledged adult. He would then himself, if so inclined, seek to become a lover of a younger beloved. Lovers were usually already married, and same-sex marriages were not legally permitted. Adult men who maintained erotic connections with other adult males were seen as violating accepted social norms. They could even find themselves mocked in comic dramas produced at large-scale public festivals. This onstage mockery could border on the explicit in language and even action. Characters in the publicly funded comic dramas freely delivered lines studded with sexually explicit language and emphasized with gestures.

No extant source reports any involvement of the adolescent Phocion with an older man, but this does not mean he had none. At the least he would have frequently observed these relationships. He would have learned that regrettable complications could emerge from such close pairings — malicious gossip and even enduring hatred were not unknown consequences of these highly personal relationships. This realization is perhaps relevant to his much-noted reluctance as an adult to engage in the intimate socializing in small groups at parties or the gossipy gatherings designated "clubs of friends" that were characteristic of the leisure of upper-class Athenian men, who were often opposed to democracy because it did not privilege them.

Another prominent form of competition among young people involved musical choruses at large public festivals. Girls could appear in group musical performances, while boys of Phocion's socioeconomic class would show off their physical fitness. These young men competed to win best in show by performing in singing and dancing groups armed as warriors prancing in formation while wearing little or no clothing. These much-attended performances provided the contestants with the experience of expressing civic and religious values in public. Above all, Phocion, like his social contemporaries, would have encountered the ubiquity of Athenian society's emphasis on vying for victory over other citizens in public activities.

Children who were fully occupied with daily physical labor and needed to earn a living, of course, had very different experiences.

Performing roles in religious rituals also served to school young people in norms of public life and the nature of core Athenian values. Singing groups often performed to praise the gods of the city-state. The songs flattered the divine beings on whose benevolence the community's well-being was believed to depend. Boys could also serve as entrails cookers at animal sacrifices honoring the gods. The youths carried the innards of the dead animal to the sacrificial fire so the pieces could be roasted. Their smoky savor then ascended to the sky to delight the deities above. In addition, pictures sculpted in stone as devotional offerings to Asclepius, the god of medicine and healing, show that children regularly accompanied their families to offer prayers and thanks for his divine medical interventions.

A child's informal training in civic and religious values mattered a great deal. Despite the absence of an official dogma informing religious belief or of a body of scriptural literature, Greeks, with the exception of the occasional atheist, agreed that human flourishing depended on their city-state as a community doing everything possible to stay on the good side of the gods. Civic politics and religion were deeply intertwined. Publicly funded temples, large-animal sacrifices, and some 120 festivals each year expressed the Athenian population's gratitude to the deities for their favor and the citizens' desire to prevent divine anger from being directed at them. These manifestations of piety in effect were prayers to the gods never to desert or punish their human devotees. Children had the importance of honoring the gods drilled into them from an early age. Over time, they would also learn that disagreements about what constituted genuine religious piety in both intellectual and ritual contexts could generate serious, sometimes even deadly, disputes. In Phocion's lifetime, the most dramatic proof was the trial of the infamously controversial Athenian Socrates. In 399, he was executed by vote of a jury of his male Athenian peers for allegedly having corrupted the young men of Athens by imbuing them with his unconventional religious and political views.

Phocion was much too young to have been aware of this controversial event when it happened, but as a later student of Plato he would have heard at first hand bitter reminiscences of the fate of Plato's famed teacher. Based on certain idiosyncratic habits Phocion adopted in his adult life, we have good reason to believe that the memory of Socrates made a huge impression on him. Other Athenians clearly noticed that Phocion, like Socrates, implicitly set himself apart from them in his public behavior. As we will see, demonstrating this sort of individuality could put a citizen's treasured status as a person belonging to the community at risk, and the consequences to his reputation could be serious. At the same time, we have no evidence that Phocion had anything other than a conventional appreciation of the importance of religious piety and honoring the gods. Views on these matters would have been especially relevant to his promotion of Athens's safety. He, like other Athenians, would have believed that maintaining the divine favor of the city-state's patron deities was an essential civic goal.

Sons were usually more welcomed in ancient Greek families than daughters because they could carry on the family name. Daughters, at least in families with sufficient resources, were expected to take a valuable dowry away with them when they became a member of their husband's family. Overall, however, the emotional experience of a boy could be uncertain in his relationship with his father. For one thing, as previously described, boys in families rich enough to have multi-chambered houses had spent the earliest years of their lives mostly in the company of women. Sons therefore saw relatively little of their fathers in the years when they first began to develop affective relations with adults in their families and other close contacts, including household slaves. And since pedagogues customarily spent more time with pre- and early adolescent children than did their fathers, a boy's strong emotional tie to another male probably more frequently emerged from this near-constant inter-action. These circumstances may have shaped Phocion's feeling of connection with his own father. Whatever their relationship was like, if Phocion's father was still alive during his son's teenage years, Phocion would have begun to spend more time with him and his father's friends and associates. Another male relative would have taken over this responsibility if Phocion's father had already died.

During this period of his life Phocion would have been exposed to a basic assumption of the child-parent relationship that pre-vailed in his society: children owed a literal debt of gratitude to their parents for raising them that had to be repaid by taking care of their parents in their later years. Children thus were responsible for practicing the habits of life that would benefit their families. They had to earn wages if they were poor. If they were well off, they had to behave conventionally in public social and religious ceremo-nies. All were supposed to show that they were ready to grow into responsible and respected citizens regardless of social status. This expectation applied to women as well as men, but in the masculine-dominated context of Greek life, male children were the first in line for paying the debt to their parents. The women whom they mar-ried were expected to help them. As in so much of Greek life, the underlying — and unassailable — principle of the parent-child rela-tionship was reciprocity. This particular reciprocal arrangement de-fined, in the philosopher Aristotle's words, the *philia* (attachment and friendly relationship) meant to exist between children and par-ents. The former were expected to regard the latter as "something good and above them."[1]

We do not know to what extent, if any, Phocion paid his debt to his parents. It does seem possible, however, that he may have felt that there was little to be repaid, at least in his relationship with his father. That is, Phocion's experience as a male child may well have later influenced the affectively remote approach to parenting that he apparently took toward his own son. The consequences, as we will see, drastically undermined their relationship during his son's youth. Their connection turned out to be so fraught that Phocion went to a startling extreme to try to discipline a son whose behavior he regarded as shameful and humiliating to his family. It seems reasonable to surmise that this failure of father-son harmony reflected Phocion's lasting memory of an unhappy relationship with his own father. In any case, it was surely true that Phocion grew up with a keen sense of the fragility of ties among people who were conventionally supposed to be on good terms with one another based on their belonging to the same family, whether that group was small or large.

In fact, the tension between Phocion and his son may also have undermined his public standing as a leader in the contentious arena of policy making in Athenian democracy—the larger family to which he was expected to belong. As Phocion's fellow countryman, orator, and political activist Aeschines (ca. 397–ca. 322) phrased it in a public speech delivered much later to criticize their shared rival, the famed orator Demosthenes (384–322), "the man who hates his child and is a bad father could never become a safe guide to the people." Whatever the details might have been concerning the relationships between Phocion and his father and Phocion and his own son, it is conceivable that this personal history was detrimental to Phocion's career. At the least, Phocion's political enemies could have cited his trouble with his son as evidence that the father was untrustworthy. We do know that Phocion fell significantly short in his understanding of how most effectively to forge positive relations with other Athenian men in the public sphere. He would have benefited from better strategies for working with others to find mutually acceptable solutions to problems affecting them all as citizens belonging to the same *polis* (city-state).[2]

Like other boys of his class, Phocion as his teenage years progressed would not have spent much time around Athenian men who had to work for a living. Greeks called their jobs artisanal occupations, by which they meant working long hours with their hands. Wealthier men instead spent much of their time exercising in the public gymnasiums, training to become effective military commanders, serving in public office in the democratic government, attending meetings of the city-state's governing Council of Five Hundred and Assembly, and conversing with other men in the open central area called the *agora* (public gathering and market space). They could attend the performances of tragedies and comedies in publicly sponsored dramatic festivals that explored thought-provoking themes about how they should behave as family members and citizens.

In the evenings, well-off males gathered at symposiums ("drinking-together parties"), at which the only women present were slave servers and hired entertainers. Adolescents were deemed too young to attend these parties as full participants in the conversations and the drinking. On occasion, however, they were allowed to observe the goings-on and answer a question or two if asked. His subsidiary role as a junior guest at these socially important gatherings would have provided an opportunity for Phocion to begin to grasp the norms of a privileged Athenian male life. He would have observed how adult men could behave when they were inebriated and not in the company of their wives. Drinking-together parties not infrequently degenerated into drunken debacles.

Later in his adult life Phocion almost always declined to join in symposiums. Similarly, he did not visit the city's public baths, where men could meet informally, as he apparently preferred to wash without any company at home. These habits strikingly set him apart from his male contemporaries whose social and economic status allowed them the privilege — and imposed the expectation — of regularly spending their time socializing with their elite peers. For example, these men often convened comradely gatherings, clubby get-togethers that provided essential mechanisms for them to make the connections that would benefit them economically and politically. In short, drinking and cavorting at symposiums and spending time with a specific group of friends were important components in demonstrating a man's belonging to his appropriate, narrow stratum of the Athenian community. Phocion shunned these conventions. In this regard he resembled the renowned fifth-century BCE Athenian leader Pericles — he too had been a member of the social elite but did not socialize according to its accepted norm.

Why these two famous Athenians made the choice to stand aloof from their fellows is not easy to determine. Phocion's adult public conduct seems to suggest that he took his distinctively unusual course as a way of avoiding accusations that his political stances were directed by the influence of rich friends. This was also said to have been Pericles' motive. They both hoped, if this were the case, to avoid identifying themselves as men who superciliously set themselves apart from the communal interests of the mass of their fellow citizens, the *demos*. In any case, Phocion consistently shunned obvious displays of excess wealth, which would have identified him with the upper-class critics of his city-state's direct democracy as the rule of the poor majority. This behavior would seem at least an attempt by Phocion to signal that he thought he belonged to the *whole* of the population.

At the same time, however, his seeming rejection of the social elite's sense of personal superiority toward less fortunate members of the Athenian demos clashed with his many in-your-face public statements denigrating the virtues and value of non-elite citizens. Such comments seem out of place for a leader who wished to communicate a firm sense of belonging to the polis. As events would prove, Phocion was sadly mistaken if he expected that his idiosyncratic behavior toward his own social equals would induce the majority of Athenian voters, all of them men, to listen calmly to his recommendations on policy when his advice conflicted with their own views. Phocion was no doubt in his own distinct way trying to demonstrate his sincerity in promoting the shared advantage of the community, but he seriously misjudged its psychological effectiveness.

One thing that Phocion did secure was his identity as a citizen who legitimately belonged to the Athenian polis, thanks to his family, who guided him successfully through the public process required to achieve that recognition. Athens's citizens especially prized their shared identity, as shown by their boasting that they were special. They insisted that Athenians were, to use their term, autochthonous: their ancestors had always inhabited the same geographical area and had never been immigrants. Citizens believed that their territory, Attica, had been their homeland from the beginning of time and that they had inherited their position of belonging to a special group.

The Athenians contrasted themselves with citizens of other city-states because those Greeks were originally foreigners who had arrived from other locations, sometimes very far away indeed. The Thebans, for example, populated a major city-state to the north of Athens that was often its rival for regional power. These Greeks said that they had come to their present location from a homeland far away in Phoenicia, a coastal region at the eastern end of the Mediterranean Sea. The Spartans, Athens's most bitter enemy for more than a century by the time of Phocion's birth, claimed descent from the famous Heracles. He had been born in Thebes to a mother who was originally from the northeast Peloponnese peninsula. The Athenians overtly prided themselves on being different in their "unlike-you-we-have-always-lived-in-the-same-location" civic identity. They saw themselves as instantiations of their ancestors both in literal location and in descent. Their sense of belonging was in this aspect rare and therefore emphatically valuable in their eyes.

By listening to his relatives and their conversations with friends, Phocion would have absorbed another important point that Athenians agreed on about their past. Their ancestors, they boasted, had created and defended their communal freedom against the attempts of other peoples to dominate them. Those aggressive enemies had sometimes been Greek, sometimes foreigners — "barbarians," as Greeks called them. This designation literally indicated only people who did not speak Greek or share Greek cultural traditions. Ethnic and racial prejudice against others, however, certainly existed in Greek thought and practice. "Barbarians" were often deemed to be inferior to Greeks in their characters and ways of life. At the same time, Greeks' evaluations of different peoples were not uniform or simple. Some "barbarians," for example, could rate as ugly, stupid, and weak from a Greek perspective. Others, however, ranked as beautiful, intelligent, and powerful. Even central tenets of Greek religion were believed to have been imported from the thought and practices of peoples in Ethiopia and India. Perceptive Greeks therefore realized that it was necessary to delve below the surface to reach reliable conclusions about the character of those they designated barbarians.

There were many diverse "barbarian" peoples in the Greeks' part of the world. They, like Greeks, were not unified, often fighting with one another as well as with Greeks. The barbarians in the north were seen by their southern Greek neighbors as being especially fierce warriors, prone to raiding their neighbors. To the east, in southwest Asia, by far the most prominent and powerful barbarians were the Persians. Their monarchs prided themselves on an ideology of cultural superiority that justified an endless pursuit of empire. The Persian kingdom dominated many groups of other "barbarians" in a vast, multi-ethnic state. How to deal with the Persian kings' unrivaled power—and later their astonishing weakening and eventual loss of it in the time of Alexander the Great—would present a quandary for Phocion throughout his adult life. What to do about Persia always loomed as an issue once he became prominent in the debates over Athenian policy.

Othering people was a tradition that also applied to Greeks thinking about Greeks. Ancient Greece was not a unified nation; it consisted of more than a thousand independent communities occupying their own territories throughout the eastern Mediterranean region. And many of these Greek states were often at war with one another. Such conflicts led Greeks to be ready to disparage not just "barbarians" but also their fellow Hellenes, to use their term. (The modern term "Greeks" comes from what the Romans called them.)

A half-century before Phocion was born, the specificity of Athens's autochthony received even greater emphasis. During the time that Pericles was the city-state's most influential political leader, the voters passed a new citizenship law, proposed by him, that required both parents to be ethnic Athenians in order for their child to be confirmed as Athenian. Previously, only the father had to be Athenian for his children to receive Athenian citizenship. Up until that time, rich men of Athens had often married women from wealthy foreign families in order to strengthen their financial resources and build profitable international connections.

Following the passage of the Periclean Citizenship Law in 451 BCE, Athenian citizenship became a matter of purity of blood. Belonging at Athens was therefore inherited, not acquired. The voters could legally bestow citizenship on foreigners, but this happened only occasionally. Such citizenship was most frequently a diplomatic honor given individual foreign potentates who had done favors for Athens and had no intention of coming to live there. In addition, political emergencies did on a couple of occasions lead to the bestowal of citizenship on the entire free population of an allied state.

The importance accorded the concept of belonging was inherent in the series of official procedures required to verify a boy's position as a legitimate family member deserving Athenian citizenship. That status entitled him to possess the legally protected identity of a member of the demos, the citizen population as a whole. Phocion's completion of this process ensured that as an adult he would possess the full political and legal rights and duties of a citizen. How to categorize the standing and scrutiny of Athenian women in terms of citizenship is a question too multi-faceted to discuss here, but in any case, girls were not included in the teenage ceremonies that guaranteed full political status to males. For boys, these rites of passage were meant to inspire a sense of belonging to the city-state because not belonging was catastrophic. There were no local or international guarantees of safety or opportunities for anyone who failed the tests. In Athens, a child denied citizenship lost all claim to full status as a human being with any rights at all.

The first step in the long process of a boy being certified as a genuine Athenian citizen who belonged to the demos took place ten days after birth. On that day, Phocion's father or, if his father had died, another male relative would have presided over a naming ceremony validating the baby's legitimacy. A child identified as the product of an extramarital affair would fail this test. Then, a little later, Phocion's status would have had to be verified once again. This vetting took place in the presence of a larger number of citizens outside the family. At a religious festival held in the fall of each year, young Athenian boys were registered in the phratry (large fraternal society with religious functions) of which their father was a member. All Athenian men of legitimate birth were expected to hold membership in one of these groups as part of the drawn-out process of securing their right of belonging to the community.

For ancient Greece, the Athenian community was large. Attica as a territory consisted of a triangular peninsula totaling about 2,500 to 3,000 square kilometers (1,000 to 1,150 square miles), depending on where its precise borders are thought to have been. Its urban center was situated near the peninsula's northwestern corner. Multiple villages spread throughout the surrounding countryside. Estimates vary of the size of the population, which seems to have recovered somewhat during the fourth century from the large-scale demographic damage done in the decades of the Peloponnesian War (431–404 BCE). One reasonable overview is that the resident population included some 30,000 to 40,000 adult males, 90,000 women and children, 40,000 metics (free foreigners with a residency permit), and 150,000 slaves, for a total of approximately 300,000+ individuals.

As a local and free member of this population, at around the age of sixteen Phocion would have undergone a coming-of-age ceremony that took place at the same religious festival at which his membership in a phratry had previously been verified. The details of this second public vetting remain obscure. Its Greek name, *koureion*, is related to getting a haircut, perhaps to indicate that the topknot characteristic of the hairstyle of young boys seen on painted Greek vases of the time was no longer appropriate for the adolescent now being publicly welcomed to a new stage of his life. That is, boys becoming men should look like one another as a way of signaling their (equality of) status and willingness to belong to their inherited group.

The final, crucial stage in belonging arrived when a boy turned eighteen. His father, if still alive, or another male relative would then present him to the male members of the father's deme, a term that derives from the same Greek word meaning "the people" (demos). Here the term indicates one of the more than 130 political districts that had been marked out within the land controlled by Athens at the end of the sixth century BCE. Demes varied greatly in the sizes of their populations and were located throughout Attica, both in the urban center and in the surrounding countryside. They were then geographically identified as located in one of three areas (city, coastal, inland) and assigned to a two-level set of administrative divisions designed so that no one area of contiguous Athenian territory could have disproportionate political power through the number of its voters or by having its demesmen filling a significantly larger or smaller number of government positions than other sections.

Phocion seems to have been from one of the several demes called Potamos; its precise location in Athenian territory is uncertain. Once his father's fellow demesmen agreed that the boy was a legitimate offspring and allowed him to share their deme identity, the next step in the process would be for his father to arrange for the city-state's Council of Five Hundred to examine the young man's suitability for citizenship. Successfully navigating this process (*dokimasia*, "being put to the test") earned the candidate official citizenship. That Phocion later went on to hold public office in Athens's government shows that he passed this test to certify his legal belonging.

The administrative arrangement of Athenian democratic government in which Phocion would eventually serve was based on ten roughly equally populated artificial divisions of demes, each of which was called a tribe (*phyle*) and named after an Athenian hero of the distant past. The tribe of which Phocion seems to have been a member based on his deme was called Leontis, named after Leos, son of the legendary singer Orpheus from the mythical past. (Leos also served as an Athenian symbol of familial patriotism because he had reportedly obeyed an oracle commanding him to sacrifice his daughters as the price for preserving the city-state.) Until the middle of the fourth century BCE, each tribe voted to elect from its members one of the ten annual civic officers called generals. After that date, all ten generals were chosen from the eligible population at large without reference to tribe. Since Phocion continued to be elected to this post throughout his long career, it is clear that for this job at least he had support from a wide swath of Athenian voters, presumably reflecting approval of his demonstrated capacity as a military leader with administrative responsibilities.

Being able to become a recognized and accepted member of a community and to feel included is key for positive human emotional development. The series of initiations experienced by young Athenian males like Phocion in the first two decades of their lives, intended to enable them to officially belong to the citizen body, would have made an indelible impression on them psychologically. In light of the anecdotal evidence for Phocion's future life, it seems that this process contributed to Phocion's often publicly antagonistic attitude toward "the people" of Athens, or "the many" as they were often called by their upper-class detractors. He apparently came to believe that simply inheriting one's civic status through one's bloodline was an inadequate criterion for belonging in the group that should possess full political rights in a Greek city-state. We can suspect that he concluded that only those whose actions and attitudes were sufficiently meritorious, sufficiently useful and good, to earn them that right, should have the power to vote on Athens's domestic and foreign policies. At the same time, however, there is no evidence that Phocion ever contemplated supporting a movement by the upper class in Athens to overturn the current system of democracy, as had happened after the Athenians' defeat in the Peloponnesian War. He most likely concluded that such drastic action would be destructive to the safety and salvation (the soteria) of Athens that he so thoroughly treasured.

It seems important to keep this apparent political inconsistency in mind when evaluating Phocion's conduct as an adult during his unprecedently long career of office-holding in Athens's government. His customary behavior predisposed the majority of his fellow citizens to suspect that he looked down on them, generating a sense of resentment on their part. What he seems not to have anticipated is that this feeling would in the long run fuel his downfall.

CHAPTER FOUR

Training for the Military

Once Phocion had been vetted to guarantee his belonging as a legitimate citizen, he would have begun an intense new phase in validating his place in the community. As an eighteen-year-old male, he would now have had to ready himself physically and psychologically to serve in Athens's military. Nothing was more important for the long-term survival of Athens (or any other Greek city-state) during this violent period of history than fielding an effective military. Not even its male citizens' participation in the political and judicial institutions of Athens's direct democracy counted for more.

The attested program of publicly mandated, formal two-year training for military service for ephebes — boys aged eighteen to twenty — came into force at some point in the fourth century BCE. Whether the Ephebic Oath quoted here and its associated training regimen were formally in existence during Phocion's teenage years in the 380s is not known. This version, attested from later in Phocion's life, dramatically expresses the paramount, eternal civic excellences that young men pledged to manifest and protect:

> I will not bring dishonor to my sacred weapons of war, and I will not desert my fellow soldier standing at my side, wherever I am stationed in the ranks. I will fight to defend both sacred and secular things and I will bequeath [to posterity] a homeland that is not smaller in size, but rather one that is larger and stronger, so far as it is in the power of myself and everyone, and I will be obedient to those who at any time govern thoughtfully, and to the established laws and to any laws that they establish in future thoughtfully. If anyone tries to abolish the laws, I will not allow it so far as it is in the power of myself and everyone, and I will honor our ancestral sacred rites. The following gods are my witnesses [a list of deities follows], the boundary markers of the homeland, the wheat, barley, vines, olive trees, and fig trees.

As the narrative of the catastrophic events that ended Phocion's life will reveal, the patriotic promise to make Athens larger and stronger was taken so seriously that it justified extreme punishment for those accused of betraying this ideal.[1]

For Phocion, the military affairs in which he personally participated during his career would play a supremely significant part in his adult life until the end of his days. They related both to his service as a commander in the field and to his role as a political figure offering advice in debates on national security. To begin consideration of this aspect of his career, I offer here relevant background on the complicated and often incompletely documented arrangements for Athens's army and navy.

The overall effectiveness of Athens's citizen militia always depended on the meshing of land and sea forces. The specifics of how this was done changed over time, including during Phocion's career.

What remained constant was that all adult male citizens healthy enough to fight were supposed to be ready for military service between the ages of eighteen and fifty-nine. Permanent-resident male foreigners were also subject to conscription, and slaves were used in special capacities. Young citizens eighteen and nineteen years old were expected to serve as infantry guards on the fortification walls of Athens's urban center and along its extra-urban borders. From the age of twenty to forty-nine, men would then serve in the front lines at home and on foreign military campaigns whenever an official decision was made to go on defense or offense in war. From fifty to fifty-nine, men could again be summoned to defend Athens as local guards and lookouts. In special cases, these older men could volunteer or be recalled to serve in the regular ranks. Generals could continue to serve at any age, no matter how advanced. As we will see, Phocion continued to serve long after his sixtieth birthday.

During Phocion's lifetime, Athens increasingly employed foreign mercenaries hired to fight for the city-state. Meanwhile, the navy grew to such a size that it required many more men than Athens could usually supply, so non-Athenians were hired in increasing numbers for that branch of the military. Free citizens in the navy also often brought along slaves they owned to row alongside them in the warships. Successfully integrating these diverse groups into a reliable and cooperative corps of men preparing for combat together presented serious challenges for the citizens such as Phocion who served as commanders in Athens's army and navy.

On land, the heavy infantry formed the largest component of the militia. These troops were known as hoplites ("those armored and armed"). Athens also mustered cavalry and mounted archers. An unmounted archer corps had existed before Phocion's early adulthood, but budgetary pressures on Athens's public finances had apparently led to its disbandment. Exact figures for the size of Athens's land forces are impossible to determine. Probably at least a third of eligible adult males were serving at any particular time throughout much of the fourth century, with heavily armored infantry outnumbering mounted warriors by about ten to one.

During the earlier decades of Phocion's life, hoplites had to possess the personal wealth necessary to purchase what they needed to fight as members of Athens's heavy infantry corps — the dangers of battle were not the only price of national service. Hoplites received a daily stipend equivalent to a day's regular wages, but until the 330s, these heavily armed infantrymen had to provide their own armor and weapons. This requirement meant that many financially less-well-off citizens could not afford to become hoplites. The outlay of capital required to acquire all this equipment was too great for a large percentage of Athenian men. They instead did their mandatory service in the navy, whose entry cost was far lower; in addition, sailors received a modest daily payment.

A hoplite's circular shield, three feet in diameter and made of wood, sometimes faced with bronze and leather, and his thrusting spear (his main battle weapon), approximately seven to eight feet long, cost about the equivalent of a month's wages from a well-paid job for a laborer. Bronze body armor for the head, arms, chest and back, and lower legs cost three times that amount. A hoplite also had to supply his own short sword and dagger to complete his standard set of weapons. These smaller arms were used when the organized phalanx battle had splintered into one-on-one combats and a soldier had no use for his larger weapons. The total weight of a hoplite's arms alone, not including his armor, could equal a third of his body weight.

The expense of readying themselves for hoplite service was probably one significant reason why by the fifth century BCE, many infantrymen had stopped wearing full-body metal armor. Instead, they substituted body protection made from lighter-weight, fibrous, thickly woven cloth. These changes greatly lessened the weight of an infantryman's equipment, making him quicker and more mobile. Equally important, the new armor also helped slow the debilitating overheating of their bodies that hoplites inevitably experienced when they were on the field of battle under Greece's often fierce sun. The revolutionary development of lighter-armed troops gained further impetus in Athens in the early fourth century. The general Iphicrates (ca. 418–ca. 353), after observing foreign warriors who fought without full body armor, introduced a special corps of foot soldiers into Athens's army that was equipped with less weighty body armor, shields made of wicker, and less cumbersome spears. The soldiers also wore lighter-weight boots to move faster.

These light infantry began to be used as a kind of quick-striking land force–cum–light-artillery. They carried throwing javelins, less heavy than the main infantry's thrusting spears, which they hurled at the enemy troops. Iphicrates probably had taken his ideas for this new kind of infantry from observing fighters from Thrace, a non-Greek region north of the lands of the mainland. In fact, the light-armed infantrymen that Athens initially deployed seem mostly to have been Thracians rather than citizens. This special role was not one that Phocion as a son from a well-off family would have filled. He could well afford to learn how to become a hoplite or a naval commander. Still, he did need to be familiar with the capabilities of light-armed troops so that when he became a general he would know how best to utilize them in battle.

If they could afford it, hoplites also brought along slaves to carry the heavy burden of their equipment while on the march to the battlefield. One man's armor, weapons, and supplies for eating and sleeping on the ground could easily weigh enough to exhaust a soldier transporting his own equipment. The effort was increased by the terrain the soldiers had to traverse. They moved from place to place mostly along rough and bumpy roadways and open territory; there were no highways. Since the price of a capable slave represented about two-thirds of an average annual salary for a working man, to say nothing of the expense of providing food and clothing for this enslaved assistant, bringing along a slave on military service was costly. A further expense for hoplites beyond providing their own armor, weapons, and slave was food for the start of the military campaign. In sum, the expense of serving in Athens's land forces was most likely prohibitive for the majority of Athenian families. This remained true even after the introduction of a daily wage paid from public funds to soldiers once they were out on campaign. Phocion's family, however, could afford all the expenses of his service as a hoplite. As a man of social and financial status he would without question have been expected to undertake the serious physical and disciplinary training needed to fight effectively as a hoplite.

As mentioned above, it is uncertain exactly how young men completed their preparation for infantry service in the era when Phocion did so. Nevertheless, even in the early fourth century, youths of Phocion's socioeconomic class were expected as teenagers to begin to practice the skills and develop the endurance they would need to serve when the city-state called on them to fight in its militia. Given the frequency of violent conflicts in which Athens was involved in Phocion's time, that call went out often. Sometimes it came on multiple occasions during a single year. Citizens with hoplite status were theoretically excused from nonstop conscription so that they could recover physically and financially from their time in the military, but there was no predicting when threats to the city-state's safety might override considerations of individual welfare. By the time he was in his mid-teens, Phocion would definitely have needed to devote considerable time and effort to readying himself for infantry service if he was called upon for hoplite service instead of that of a naval officer.

Boys like Phocion who came from financially comfortable families could develop their physical fitness in the various private gymnasiums of Athens. In addition, they had to find ways to gain experience in using their weapons when they were formed up in the close battle order in which hoplites fought. Organizing this latter type of demanding training would have required cooperation among the families with the finances to provide hoplites. In whatever way Phocion received the necessary instruction, he would have had to learn to handle a spear and shield so that he could repel enemies in the heat of battle without colliding with the soldiers who were lined up with him in the close-order rank-and-file formation of an infantry phalanx. For offense, he had to concentrate on managing his long and heavy thrusting spear with his right arm while carrying a bulky shield on his left. For offense and defense, he had to practice lining up as precisely as possible in a large formation.

Hoplite formations fought as units whose constituent soldiers were trained to keep their internal spatial locations stable with respect to one another and avoid dissolving into crowds of undisciplined individuals in a disorganized melee. So to be able to meet his civic responsibility if he had to serve as a hoplite, Phocion would have had to master the considerable challenge of moving in unison with other heavy infantrymen while carrying his heavy weapons and armor in a well-ordered charge against the ranks of the enemy force. If those opponents were Greeks, they were likely to be aligned similarly. In other words, Phocion would have had it impressed upon him that safety in war depended on working well with other people.

Phocion's military training would also teach him that as a hoplite on the battlefield he had to struggle not only against enemy soldiers but also against his own fright, heat, and fatigue. And he had to endure all these under the pressure of the unrelenting stress of literally putting his life on the line. It was risk both at the end of an enemy's sharp-pointed weapon and from being sold into slavery if captured. Phocion thereby would have learned that he would experience enormous psychological pressure to think both of himself and of his fellow soldiers when things went sideways on the field of combat, as they not infrequently did.

Through his hoplite training and experience Phocion would also come to understand the serious difficulties that infantry battles created for commanders. He would have seen that there was a desperate need for generals to be effective, persuasive, and perspicacious leaders. Commanders of infantry could do little to direct the action in a battle once combat began. Communication with troops was almost impossible in the confusion of clashing armies. With at best a loud trumpeter and signal flags with which to transmit simple directions or messengers to carry instructions to other parts of the battlefield, a general in Phocion's time faced formidable obstacles in reacting to unexpected situations. Often the best that commanders could do tactically in the moment was keep some of their forces ready to change positions during the battle according to how the momentum of the conflict was proceeding. In the best case, they could then send troops into the fight at what they deemed to be a crucial point for tipping the balance toward victory for their side. If their opponents seemed to be winning the day, on the other hand, these soldiers could help their beleaguered comrades retreat to safety.

Above all, Phocion learned that generals had to lead from the front—literally if possible, but certainly in terms of being seen by their men to be on the scene and at risk. Effective leaders could not station themselves at a safe distance from those they were directing into harm's way. Building morale for his troops under fire was a crucial psychological task for an infantry commander. A Greek infantry force that lost its formation and discipline during a battle had no chance of prevailing and often guaranteed its members' destruction. In addition, commanders' performance in the field was constantly scrutinized after the fact by their fellow citizens in Athens. Failure to succeed often led to legal prosecutions threatening drastic punishment, regardless of whether the commander was personally responsible for what had happened. Whereas monarchs, such as the Persian or Macedonian kings, had immunity from personal direct consequences for military defeats, Athenian generals knew exactly what sort of retribution awaited them if their missions disappointed their fellow citizens. Phocion could have observed this treacherous possibility as a youngster. Later in life, he would sadly gain direct experience of how brutally Athens's citizens might punish officials whose performance disappointed them.

Serving in the cavalry of Athens was regarded as a social distinction because it was even more expensive to fill a place in this mounted force than to become a fully equipped hoplite. Phocion possessed the wealth needed to serve as a cavalryman instead of a hoplite, but we have no surviving evidence to indicate whether he ever did so. At this period, cavalrymen had to provide not only their arms (spears were the main offensive weapons) and armor, but also the horses they rode and the attendants who took care of their mounts. These specially chosen animals had to be fed, cared for, and trained for action. Then they had to perform under the demanding circumstances of battle, which often took them far from home. The financial elite of Athens regularly kept horses on the properties in the countryside outside the city that most of them possessed in addition to a residence in the urban center. They could therefore furnish their own mounts for cavalry service.

By Phocion's time, however, in order to enroll the thousand or so cavalrymen that Athens customarily fielded, it had become necessary to offer a loan from public funds to potential candidates so they could purchase horses — evidently the number of sufficiently rich Athenians had taken a hit after the wars of the late fifth and early fourth centuries. The loan was to be repaid only when the cavalryman retired from active service, usually some ten or fifteen years later. Cavalry training and service were evidently too physically demanding and time-consuming for older men. The mounted corps of archers, which numbered around two hundred, received horses at state expense, presumably so that its members could be drawn from the largest possible demographic. Athens's rich families now constituted a smaller minority of the total citizen body than in the glory days of the city-state in the mid-fifth century. Cavalry and mounted archers were paid a higher daily wage than the infantry, and it included the days during which they were not actually out on campaign.

In sum, what we know for certain about Athens's land forces is that troops found it challenging to achieve the goals of military expertise expected of them. And this is to say nothing of the time required for effective training, during which those who needed to work at a day job to help support their families obviously had to take a loss in that income. Becoming an effective member of Athens's citizen militia called for a personal commitment that was far from easy.

But it was Athens's navy, as it had developed in the fifth century, that came to be the military force requiring by far the most men. Each of the city-state's largest warships, called triremes ("ships with three levels of rowers"), was propelled into battle by a crew of 200, of whom 170 were rowers. Public funds paid for building these complex vessels, but funding their expensive operating costs was a civic responsibility of the rich. The number of Athens's triremes varied over time, but battle fleets usually consisted of at least scores of triremes. Athens's full complement of such ships could at times reach into the hundreds. This meant that the Athenian navy always needed to assemble a complement of men numbering in the tens of thousands. Since serving as an infantry or a cavalry soldier involved considerable personal expenditures, the majority of Athenian male citizens either preferred, or could literally only afford, to fulfill their military responsibilities by serving as rowers in the navy. The only costs that rowers had to meet were for a cushion on which to sit and a leather rowlock to keep their oar in position. Each rower handled a separate long oar.

Triremes used sails for traveling from point to point before and after actual combat, but the sails were lowered during sea battles. Then it became the exhausting duty of the rowers, all stationed below the top deck, to propel the ship as fast as possible toward the enemy's line of ships. The goal of the attack was either to sail at speed close alongside an enemy warship to shear off its oars or to crash head-on into it to punch a hole through its hull and swamp the boat. Triremes were built with bronze-reinforced rams protruding from their bows at the waterline for the latter tactic, which was especially perilous. The ship doing the ramming had to be able to reverse in order to disengage from the collision to prevent becoming stuck in the broken timbers of its impaled enemy. Rowing in a trireme was therefore extremely challenging. It required strength, endurance, obedience to orders, and courage.

By Phocion's early adulthood, the Athenian navy was of a size that needed many more rowers than the citizen body could supply. Foreigners were therefore hired in large numbers. Slaves seem also to have been common as trireme crew members. Like hoplites, rowers, both Athenian and foreign, received a daily wage from public funds. Inscriptions show that some Athenians who owned male slaves enrolled themselves as rowers and then brought along these human possessions so that as owners they could collect their servants' wages.

As Phocion and his contemporaries knew all too well, a strong navy needed so many men not only to project military power but also and always to protect the importation by sea via privately owned merchant ships of the food and timber on which their survival depended. Grain provided the main source of calories for most Athenians, and imported wheat was more desirable than home-grown barley. As Demosthenes commented in the mid-350s, "We use much more imported grain than anybody else." Without regular delivery by cargo ships of these vital materials from coastal regions of the Black Sea and the Mediterranean, the Athenians would perish. The merchant ships depended on the navy to defend them from pirates, a constant scourge on sea-borne commerce unless it could be deterred by the presence of warships overseeing maritime trade routes to Athens.[2]

Consequently, the Athenians' dependence on resources from abroad meant that doing everything possible to maintain a large navy became a necessary and constant focus of their public policy and finances. Providing enough qualified trireme commanders (trierarchs) to achieve this goal was a crucial need. Meeting it was challenging because the qualifications for serving as a trierarch were not only military but also heavily financial. A naval commander was required to pay for the costs of outfitting and maintaining his trireme during a year's campaigning. That cost could be astronomical for an individual, in the neighborhood of the equivalent of fifteen years' wages for workmen earning average compensation. As a result, only Athens's financial elite could afford to serve as trierarchs. By Phocion's time, the burden had become so heavy that arrangements were made for citizens to share the cost of filling this crucial military office. That Phocion was able to serve as a trierarch when he was only in his mid-twenties attests to the substantial wealth that he inherited from his family.

CHAPTER FIVE

Learning About Athenian Democracy

During the period in which Phocion would have became actively engaged in physical and military training, he would also begin to learn about the structure of the democratic government of Athens in which he as a male citizen would be expected to participate once he turned eighteen. This knowledge would have initially come to him as he spent more and more time outside his household in the company of his male relatives and their friends. Reflecting their status as members of the propertied classes, these men went about their days managing their assets, chatting with their friends in the open space of the agora and the covered halls dotting its borders, going to gymnasiums and bathhouses, serving as members of government councils, participating in Assembly meetings, and attending symposiums later in the day. Phocion would also have been in close contact with other Athenian young men of his age group while they worked together on improving their physical fitness in preparation for eventual military service. In their conversations with one another they would have shared what they were learning – or believed they were learning – about the responsibilities of an active adult Athenian citizen in a direct democracy.

It is not certain whether in the early fourth century BCE young men could begin attending the Assembly as eligible voters as soon as they turned eighteen. By the 330s, they had to wait until they were twenty and had completed their training as ephebes. Whichever was the case for Phocion, he needed to learn how Athens's democracy worked. Once he officially became an adult old enough for participation in government, he was expected to attend as often as he could meetings of the Assembly, the venue where the most important decisions concerning the governing of Athens were determined.

The Assembly formed the ultimate decision-making institution of Athens's democracy. Its votes decided the city-state's policies directing both domestic and international affairs and, as we shall see, oversaw the procedure for making laws. There were no elected delegates to the Assembly, as there are in the legislatures of modern representative democracies. A literally direct democracy, the Athenian government allowed all male citizens of the required age (who had not forfeited their civic rights as punishment for illegal conduct) to attend Assembly meetings and cast votes. The voters were making decisions that directly affected themselves. Above all, when Athenian men voted that Athens should go to war, they were in fact voting to send themselves into battle and risk their own lives. Their participation in direct democracy was vivid and personal.

The first six thousand eligible men to attend an Assembly meeting received a stipend from public funds roughly equivalent to a worker's average daily wage, an innovation of the 390s to encourage attendance. This allowance meant that no one was deterred from participating in the Assembly because he could not afford to go a day without wages. In this way in particular, Athenian democracy was organized to maintain its commitment to "equality in citizenship" (*isonomia*).

By the mid-fourth century, the Assembly regularly convened forty times a year, though additional meetings could be called at any time to deal with urgent issues. Its usual meeting place was an open space atop the Pnyx Hill below the Acropolis in downtown Athens. This area was created to allow large gatherings of citizens to listen to speeches and then cast their votes on the issues being debated. Anyone, including women, children, and foreigners, could congregate outside the area formally designated for meetings and listen to the speeches. Meetings commenced at daybreak with a sacrifice to the gods, whose goodwill always had to be sought as the basis for the community's safety. Then a public announcer said a prayer and proclaimed a curse on any speaker who led the people astray. This latter proclamation emphasized the point that citizens whom the Assembly judged to have recommended harmful or corrupt decisions could expect official retribution. Curses were taken very seriously in ancient Greece as dangerous spells, and this officially pronounced curse points to how and why the majority felt justified in imposing harsh penalties on leaders who, they believed, had failed them. The Assembly's predisposition to harsh penalties was going to prove fatally relevant to Phocion at the end of his life.

The deliberations at meetings of the Assembly began when the announcer cried, "Who wishes to speak?" By Phocion's time, precedence in addressing the assembled voters was no longer extended to speakers over the age of fifty, as it had been in the past. Now anyone could mount the podium, so long as he stuck to the subjects that had been approved ahead of time for discussion in that particular meeting. This equality in speaking functioned as an unassailable principle of Athens's equality in citizenship. In fact, however, the overwhelming majority of the thousands in attendance never came forward to give a speech — addressing the Athenian Assembly took formidable abilities and a willingness to withstand blunt and loud rejection. As we will see, Phocion only rarely subjected himself to this emotionally demanding experience. Despite his deep interest in the political policies being debated in the Assembly, he refrained from making speeches there on any regular basis.

For anyone who did address the Assembly, it was necessary to be able to speak loudly and clearly for the whole of his speech. It was truly challenging to make oneself audible to the huge number of people outside, where even a slight breeze could impede the clarity of a speaker's voice, to say nothing of the incidental noise created by members of such a large audience as they shuffled, sniffled, and exchanged comments with one another. Speaking to the Athenian Assembly in an effective fashion required a vocal power that most people could not physically produce, or not for long. Expressing opinions on controversial issues in the Assembly — without notes — also required fortitude because its members frequently shouted out disagreements and insults toward speakers (foreshadowing the currently emerging trend on the floor of the U.S. Congress). Once the speeches ended, voters raised their hands to be counted. Secret ballots were used only when important questions seemed likely to be closely contested.

By observing the Assembly in action during these years of his youth, Phocion would have learned a great deal about the intense effort and implacable facade of equanimity it would take for him to speak up in the Assembly when he considered an issue pressing enough for him to present his own views, regardless of how harshly they might be received.

The structure and procedures of Athens's government that Phocion came to understand were far from simple. Athens's most important government body besides the Assembly was the council made up of five hundred male citizens. Known in Greek as the *boule* (will, deliberation, reflection), it is commonly referred to today as the Council of Five Hundred. Its members had important responsibilities, from determining the agendas for the measures to be discussed and voted on at Assembly meetings, to advising on and managing the city-state's foreign relations and overseeing its financial administration. This body therefore strongly influenced Athenian politics. Its members met every non-festival day because they had so many duties, including oversight of Athens's many other officials. The council's members, who had to be at least thirty years old, were selected in a lottery held each year among the men who voluntarily presented themselves in their deme as willing to do council service. A man could be selected for the Council of Five Hundred only twice in his lifetime, and he could not serve two years in a row, a provision that reflected the Athenians' emphasis on inducing as many citizens as possible to participate in government.

Council members received a daily allowance, but it seems that there were often difficulties in collecting a sufficient pool of volunteers. For the most part, the wealthy were more willing to shoulder the burden of council service. Presumably they found it easier to maintain their prosperity without being constantly present on their properties, which would be managed by hired workers and slaves. Men of lesser means evidently could not maintain their standard of living if they had to be away from their occupations every working day of the year. As a member of the class that could comfortably give its time to the council, Phocion would have volunteered to serve. We know that he did so at least once, at a critical time in Athenian history in the mid-330s.

The Council of the Five Hundred played a key role in the passage of new laws because once the Assembly accepted a speaker's proposal for legislation, the councilors deliberated to determine when and in what formulation the change should be considered by the group called lawmakers (*nomothetai*). This legislative committee, whose number was decided by the Assembly, was chosen by lot from the six thousand citizens over thirty years of age who had also been selected by a lottery to serve as jurors in Athens's courts for the current year. The lawmakers then held a session lasting one day that itself resembled a trial. There the proposer of the law first spoke in its favor and then five men designated by the Assembly opposed the change. The justification for this adversarial procedure was that any innovation in the laws was treated as an attack on Athens's existing statutes, which deserved respect because of their age. A majority vote of the lawmakers decided the case, and their arguments often fueled heated feelings among the two sides. From observing these tense confrontations, Phocion must have learned how hostile the feelings of conflict among his fellow citizens could become in disagreements about traditional standards and norms. He would therefore be under no illusion that politics in fourth-century Athens was anything other than an enterprise involving serious personal risk.

Phocion would have absorbed a similarly unsettling lesson from observing trials in Athens's courts. There were several kinds of courts, of which the most popular and democratic were the *dikasteria* (institutions for determining justice and setting affairs in order). These judicial organs of government could exercise as much power as the Assembly in affecting Athens's political policies and social stability because many of their cases involved political charges. The dikasteria could decide disputes over incompetency in office, misuse of public funds, and, most serious, treason. Athenian courts had no judges, state prosecutors, public defenders, or private attorneys. The jurors reached verdicts on their own after listening to the accused and their accusers speaking on their own behalf. Defendants and accusers also often called on their own supporters to speak. Speeches had time limits, trials ended within one day, and jurors received a stipend for each day they spent in court. Juries numbered between 201 and 2,501 and were assembled on the day of the trial from the 6,000 jurors in the jury pool.

As in the meetings of the lawmakers, court speeches could be fierce. Before reaching their decisions, jurors swore to abide by the laws or, if no law addressed the situation, to remain impartial. They did not, however, pledge to remain quiet. The Athenians in fact used the term *thorubos* (shouted disagreement, moaning) to describe not just heckling in the Assembly but also the uproar that jurors often created to signal their opposition to what speakers were arguing. Since contentious trials were frequent and open to the public, Phocion as an adult acquired plentiful knowledge of how intense and consequential the Athenian court system could be. Like others with eyes on public service, he fully grasped that embarking on that sort of career meant inserting himself into a precarious environment. In short, prominent public figures involved in Athenian politics had a great deal to worry about — they had to worry about not only their city-state's safety but also their own. The risk in taking this course was clear. As is apparent from his later career, Phocion evidently thought that he had to accept the potential danger in order to satisfy his personal sense of commitment to his *idea* of what a democratic city-state should be.

Athens also had a legally empowered group called the Council of the Areopagus, named for the hill next to the Acropolis on which this council met. It consisted of men who had previously served as one of the annual officials known as archons ("rulers, commanders"). These councilors remained members for life. Our best guess from demographic data is that membership hovered at about 150 former archons. The origins of this group of elder statesmen dated back to the deepest prehistory of Athenian democracy in the time of the famous founder Solon (archon in 594/3). At that date, the council had authority over certain types of cases, acted as the ultimate guardian of the laws, and served to rein in officials and keep Athens's government from adopting overly radical – meaning strongly democratic – policies.

During the fifth century BCE, however, the Council of the Areopagus's powers of oversight were severely reduced, especially by an enactment in 462/1, so that it became no more than a court for trying cases of homicide, wounding, and arson, as well as certain religious offenses. During Phocion's lifetime, most likely beginning in the 340s, the Council of the Areopagus gradually regained much of its original supervisory status, from checking on officials' administration of the laws to supervising all the sanctuaries of the gods in Attica to prosecuting offenses both criminal and civil. Above all, this council served as a conservative brake on what some elite Athenians regarded as excessively self-serving policies of the people. This development is important for Phocion's story because it clearly underlines the growing, and eventually explosive, tensions in his lifetime between what we might anachronistically refer to as conservative versus radical sentiments among the citizens of Athenian democracy. Since Phocion apparently never held the position of archon, he did not become a member of this council, but we do know that he had significant interactions with it late in his career.

To be chosen for the offices Phocion filled throughout his career, he first had to reach the age of thirty. It is revealing that the age at which men could serve in the top offices in Athens's democracy corresponds to that at which modern research in cognitive science shows that the neurons in the male brain become fully connected. Men younger than thirty have not yet reached their full mental capacity, and long experience had evidently taught the Athenians this fact of human development. A multitude of male officials above this age, some seven hundred, carried out diverse functions in their government by serving annual terms. Hundreds of officials (magistrates, as modern scholars misleadingly call them) were responsible for carrying out decisions of the Assembly and the councils, from overseeing maintenance of public facilities to administering public finance to controlling trading in Athens's open-air markets to filling high military commands, and much more. The board of ten archons was among the groups fulfilling a diverse range of responsibilities that included religious, judicial, and lawmaking duties. The archons also monitored the functioning of Athenian government in general.

The overwhelming majority of Athens's officials were chosen by lot, in keeping with the principle of involving as many different citizens as possible in active roles in government. It seems probable that in the fourth century most of these officials received daily pay, for it is unlikely that enough men could have been found to fill so many positions if only those with sufficient private resources could serve. Candidates also underwent public scrutiny for their suitability for office before beginning their annual terms. As members of large boards they could not act solely on their own in important matters. They also had to pass a final examination of their conduct at the end of their year in service and might have to respond to accusations of malfeasance during their time in office. Penalties imposed for conduct judged corrupt or inadequate were often severe.

About a hundred Athenian officials were elected rather than selected by lottery. This more deliberative procedure reflected the importance attached to their duties. By Phocion's time, the posts these officials filled included those related to the city-state's most significant financial administrative tasks, those in charge of certain sacred affairs related to the official worship of the gods, the superintendent of the civic water supply, and top military commands. It was service in this last capacity that would distinguish Phocion. As already mentioned, he won election to the high office of general (*strategos,* "leader of a group, of a military force") forty-five times. This total well outstripped the number of generalships held by any predecessor in that office, including the famous Pericles. Since Phocion could not be elected a general until he was at least thirty years old, and he died when in his early eighties, he must have been elected to this annual high office at the astonishing rate of more than 80 percent of the time.

Generals could be tasked with a number of diverse responsibilities. Athens's generals served as members of a board, in their case numbering ten men. They were responsible for calling up male citizens and metics for military service, organizing the maintenance and command of warships, bringing to trial and judging men accused of desertion or evasion of military service, and resolving disputes among members of the financial elite about who should hold the post of trierarch and therefore also pay for the cost of operating a warship. During Phocion's lifetime, it became the rule to assign one strategos to be in charge of Athens's hoplite forces, one to oversee the trierarchs, one to oversee the defense of urban Athens and its surrounding territory in Attica, and two to ensure the defense of the port of Piraeus, whose full functioning was essential for both the operations of the navy and the continuation of the supply chains of Athens's exports and imports. The other five generals stayed available for other assignments.

The number of times a strategos could hold this annual high office was unlimited, a reflection of the electorate's understanding that experience helped make better generals. Even though the generals served as members of a board, when they were commanding forces in the field they had extensive individual authority and corresponding responsibilities. They were subject to very strict review of their performance by the people. The Assembly held a vote ten times each year on whether the generals were performing their duties satisfactorily. If anyone was voted a failure, he was deposed from office and usually then subjected to a trial by jury. And even if a general was not accused of malfeasance at one of these votes during his term of office, he still had to undergo a strict official examination of his conduct at the end of the year before he could lay down his position without penalty. Generals found guilty of failure to perform satisfactorily could be punished even up to the death penalty by vote of their fellow citizens.

Phocion evidently retained a deep skepticism about the wisdom of such oversight by ordinary citizens. Once when he received a positive response from the voters in the Assembly to a speech he had just made, he sarcastically remarked, "Did I somehow not understand that I was saying something bad?" On another occasion, he responded to abusive comments directed at him in the Assembly by replying, "I have given [the voters] lots of fine and advantageous advice, but they are not persuaded by me." And one time he remarked that even though a policy decision he had opposed had turned out favorably, things would have gone much better if his advice had been followed instead.[1]

Finally, any consideration of the development of the attitudes that shaped Phocion's decisions during his public career must include the fact that during his later teen years and into his twenties he also enjoyed an elite form of higher education. This more formal type of instruction set him apart from most Athenian males, whose "higher education" consisted of following around their older male relatives and interacting with contemporaries. But the details we have about Phocion's intellectual environment hint at answers to some of the most difficult questions concerning why he conducted himself as he did as a political leader in Athens. This formative time of his life probably contributed significantly to his adoption of what seem to have become underlying principles: our perception of reality is permeated by persistent ambiguity, the multitude of men are inadequately equipped to become thoughtful political agents in a direct democracy, and a leader of excellence must recognize the necessity of pursuing the shared advantage and benefit for himself and others regardless of the danger to him personally.

Phocion received this elite education from the man who would become Athens's most renowned intellectual, Plato (ca. 424/3–347). Plutarch says that Phocion was still young when he began studying with Plato, so their connection probably began in the mid-380s. This was when Plato opened what would grow into his famed school at Athens. Plato began gathering together men (only two women seem ever to have been included) of all ages at a complex in suburban Athens to discuss and explore a wide range of subjects. He emphasized the study of mathematics but expanded the group's discussions to include what today would count as philosophical topics. These ranged from abstract reasoning to moral and political questions. Plato's school came to be known as the Academy, which strictly speaking is a topographical indicator for an area of land associated with the memory of a hero from ancient Athenian legend named Academos. Physically arranged with access to outdoor and indoor areas for conversation, Plato's Academy was not a prep school or college or graduate school in any contemporary sense. From an institutional point of view, it was an informal association with no rigid admissions process, no fees, no enforced attendance policy, and no academic degrees.

The Academy evolved into a group of intellectually inclined individuals whom Plato inspired to talk with him. Its membership changed over time as people came and went. Most students probably attended for relatively limited periods off and on as their other commitments allowed, and few stayed on to become full-time researchers or philosophers. Plato apparently did assume a leadership role as *scholarch* (archon in charge of leisure; *schole* in Greek means leisure, time spent without having to labor at a job, and is the root of the English word *school*). This title reflected the reality that those associating with Plato at the Academy had to come from well-off families because they would not have had the free time to participate if they depended on laboring for their living. Plato supported a group spirit of a shared identity by hosting dinner parties and performing shared sacrifices to Apollo and the Muses. He also placed a portrait of his controversial mentor Socrates in a building on the grounds.

In this period Plato was already regularly working on composing and revising the written treatises known as his dialogues that ensured his lasting reputation. There were no official Academy publications or formal policy recommendations. Other than insisting that his companions at the Academy take seriously the study of mathematics, Plato imposed no rigid curriculum. The Academy did, however, soon became renowned for the high-powered conversations it inspired. Still, not everyone looked up to Plato, the leader of a company of financially secure men with so much leisure they could afford to chat away their days in his company as philosophers. Indeed, the authors of the kind of raucous comedies popular on the Athenian stage mocked the Academy in their productions. A play by Amphis, for example, included this line: "Oh Plato, all you know how to do is frown by raising your eyebrows together like two snails!"[2]

As a member of Athens's elite class, Phocion was able to join the Academy once he secured Plato's approval. He was most likely introduced by Chabrias (ca. 420–356), a contemporary of Plato's who would later be important to Phocion's early military career. No formal textbooks existed for members of the Academy to study. The only available written materials were manuscripts of works of various kinds, from mathematics to philosophy to history. Receiving the most discussion, we can imagine, were subjects for what would become Plato's dialogues. These were composed to showcase interlocutors expressing divergent opinions, and their discussions often reached no agreement but rather a state of *aporia* (no way forward). Plato expected and accepted that the discussions at the Academy would reflect a diversity of views not necessarily agreeing with his own.

In fact, the compositional structure characteristic of Plato's written works reveals that he emphasized how difficult it was for human beings to discern the ultimate reality of, basically, everything. That reality he called the Forms, by which he meant divinely created immortal perfections that existed in a sphere accessible only to those with exceptional intellectual capacity. The Forms were only and always imperfectly embodied in what human beings experienced as the world of the senses. Moreover, people could only hope to perceive this reality as a shadowy reflection seeping into their limited understanding. For Plato, the Forms had been created by a divine force he denominated as the Good. Precisely what constituted the Good in either divine or human terms apparently remained a subject for deep discussion and refinement over time. The idea that somewhere there existed an enduring truth was meant to spur human beings to strive for excellence and the Good—while never forgetting how deceptive were the surface appearances of all human interactions.

Plato saw the Good in politics as belonging neither to the rule of an authoritarian ruler nor to democratic governments conducted by the many. Rather, it required political agents to strive to act with "rectitude and justice" (*dikaiosune*) rather than from raw self-interest. Plato had personal experience in the reality that achieving this ideal was far easier said than done. Before he founded the Academy, he had sailed to Syracuse, a prosperous city-state in Sicily, at the invitation of its tyrant Dionysius I. When Plato publicly and frankly expressed his disgust at what he saw as the cruelty and immoral sensuality of his host's rule, Dionysius had Plato sold into slavery. A fellow philosopher, Anniceris, perhaps from the Greek city of Cyrene in Libya, purchased Plato's freedom, allowing him to return to Athens. When Plato's friends offered to repay Anniceris, the generous liberator told them to give the money to Plato instead to finance what he needed to maintain his Academy.

Plato's views on the type of people qualified to exercise control in government certainly were influenced by history. He was born to a well-off Athenian family from the social elite, and he grew up during a tumultuous period in the last decades of the fifth century when democratic and oligarchic factions competed for control of the city-state, sometimes violently. Notable works of Plato deal with the questions of the best structure for government and who should have the most decision-making power on issues affecting individuals and communities politically and morally. This emphasis suggests that his memories of his early real-world experiences influenced his philosophical thinking on these topics.

Plato's reflections on Athens's history during the early decades of his life would have generated discussions in the Academy that supplemented other discussions there focused on abstract philosophical questions. Before Plato's birth, Athens in the second and third quarters of the fifth century had prided itself on being the most powerful city-state in mainland Greece. It gloried in exercising domination over allies who as members of the Delian, or First Athenian, League paid to support its large navy. The Athenians' prominence and pride were broken, however, by their humiliating loss to the Spartans in the generation-long Peloponnesian War (431–404, named after Sparta's allies, the so-called Peloponnesians, most of whose city-states were located, like Sparta, in the Peloponnese peninsula of southern Greece). At the end of this war the young Plato experienced dire examples of how both the many and the social elite could betray the Good.

First, in 406/5, during a period of extreme stress for Athens near the end of the war, Plato witnessed the verdict of a jury at the trial of eight Athenian military commanders. They were in court for having failed to save fellow citizens who had drowned when a severe storm suddenly arose at the end of an Athenian naval victory off the Arginusae Islands (three islands close to the western coast of Turkey) in the northeastern Aegean. The violent weather had prevented their rescue. Although Athens's legal procedure expressly required individuals at risk of capital punishment to be tried separately, the Assembly, acting as a jury court in the name of the people, ignored this law and condemned the commanders to death as a group.

Then, in 404, Athens was defeated and had to surrender to the Spartans, who stationed a garrison of Spartan soldiers on the Acropolis. A couple of Plato's older, socially elite relatives became leaders in the Athenian cabal or junta now appointed by the vengeful Spartans to rule Athens. Known later as the Thirty Tyrants, this oligarchic faction betrayed its claim to provide a government that would be morally superior to direct democracy. Instead, the Thirty ruthlessly persecuted personal enemies on trumped-up charges and looted their property for personal gain. Murders cloaked as politically justified executions became a mainstay of the Thirty's reign of terror. Socrates, no fan of democracy, nevertheless at a crucial juncture refused the Thirty's order to assist in its depredations. Plato, who had become embroiled with the regime through relatives who took prominent or leading roles in the conspiracy, dissociated himself from the group in disgust at its manifest hypocrisy. The Thirty Tyrants had dramatically demonstrated just how far human beings, even those identifying themselves as superior, could diverge in evil from the divinely good Forms that they professed to embody in their nondemocratic system of governing.

In 403, armed resistance by Athenians both elite and poor, supported by Thebes, succeeded in overthrowing these Spartan-supported oligarchs in a bitter if brief civil war. When democracy was restored at Athens, an amnesty for war crimes was proclaimed in an attempt to foster a nonviolent political climate. But Plato once again learned in a painfully personal way how likely appearances were to be deceptive. Despite the amnesty, some citizens still sought retribution against the men whom they held responsible for the horrors of the Thirty Tyrants. Those blamed included Plato's mentor Socrates because he had been a friend or teacher of some of the worst of that vicious regime. To get around the ban on prosecuting war criminals, citizens accused Socrates of not respecting Athens's gods and corrupting the city-state's youth. Socrates' defense speech at his trial in 399 became renowned through its representations by Plato and his contemporary and fellow student Xenophon. Both wrote works known as *Apology* (*apologia* is Greek for "self-defense"), which offer somewhat differing accounts of how Socrates responded to the accusations. In both he defiantly denied the charges, insisting that he had always striven to promote excellence and dikaiosune — rectitude and justice — among his fellow citizens. He said he instructed his followers to contemplate the ambiguities that needed to be resolved to achieve those goals. Socrates' defense failed in a close vote, and he was condemned to death. Infamously, he had to pay for the hemlock potion by which he died and to administer this poison himself.

The trial and execution of Socrates confirmed Plato in the view that democracy could never be the best form of government. He subsequently discussed his position extensively in dialogues that became famous, above all his *Republic*. Its arguments portrayed "the many" as simply incapable of understanding and putting into action the conditions necessary to instantiate the Good in a world permeated by uncertainty. Only philosophically trained thinkers who were fully conscious of the ambiguous complexity of reality could ever hope to lead a government with the required level of awareness and selflessness. And it was incumbent upon them never to yield to the unthinking passions of the many, regardless of the danger to themselves.

The intellectual and historical lessons that Phocion absorbed at the Academy seem essential to understanding why he often expressed publicly such highly critical judgments of the majority of his fellow citizens. They also suggest why he defiantly supported policies that at crucial points contradicted the preferences of the many. In a real sense, he lived his life exemplifying what the character Socrates in one dialogue called the task of doing what was right but always with good sense and prudence — or at least that must be how Phocion saw his conduct. Perhaps he would have done well to remind himself that Socrates characteristically phrased this concept of behavior as a question — What in the world is it? This was a question that the philosopher always insisted he was unable to answer fully.

Phocion kept up his engagement with the elite intellectual atmosphere of the Academy. He stayed in touch with Plato throughout the latter's life, and in his later years he was friends with Xenocrates of Chalcedon, who became Plato's second successor as head of the Academy in 339/8. Ultimately, Phocion's solution to the challenge of doing what was right and being guided by good sense seems to have been a commitment to promote what he saw as the path to safety for Athens. To achieve that shared advantage and benefit, he lived simply and with integrity, displayed idiosyncratic initiative in war, and used direct, confrontational speech in politics. As he once said, he chose to suffer evil himself rather than "do evil to the Athenians." This decision seems to reflect the influence on him of study with Plato: not because Phocion became a philosopher but rather because he became a leader aspiring to do things in an unconventional way based on his deep reflections on how political decisions should be made. Those thoughts privileged the preservation of order and safety in the face of persistent ambiguity and danger in Athens's international affairs. But even his commitment to supporting what he saw as the absolute good for his polis failed to save him from arousing suspicion among the many of Athens concerning the depth of his sense of belonging to a common polity with them.[3]

CHAPTER SIX

Starting a Public Career

P hocion was in his twenties when in the late 380s or early 370s he embarked on the career of public service that Athenians expected from their elite but did not always receive. Not every Athenian young man aspired to a career in which he might become ever more involved in Athens's affairs, beyond the mandated minimum military and civic responsibilities. More than a few quiet Athenians chose to remain as apolitical as possible, while some irresponsible citizens shirked their civic duties altogether. Phocion was not among these groups. His long service in government suggests that he saw himself as living the Platonic ideal of a life of rectitude and justice by participating in a governmental system that he nevertheless criticized because it was controlled by the votes of the many. He evidently saw it as his duty to promote the safety of his less than ideal city-state during increasingly turbulent times.

To understand Phocion's public career, we need to start by analyzing what at this stage of his life he would have known about Athens's current situation and what he thought needed to be done about it. To begin with, he would have realized that he had been born into a deeply unsettled political environment. His birth followed soon after the deadly civil war provoked by the oligarchic regime of the Thirty Tyrants. And that regime was itself a product of the disaster for the Athenians that ended the Peloponnesian War. Their defeat came after twenty-seven years of off-and-on struggle had decimated their population, drained their financial resources, and aroused fiercely hostile emotions between the elite citizenry, who favored an oligarchy, and the many, who made up the democracy.

These trying times were considerably worsened by the harsh punishments the Spartans imposed on their defeated enemies, even beyond the disabling of Athens's democracy. Perhaps the worst of these additional penalties was the forced demolition of the tall stone fortifications called the Long Walls, which connected the walled city center of Athens with its main port at Piraeus some six miles to the southwest. The Long Walls had provided Athens with life-saving protection because they prevented enemies from setting up a block-ade between port and city to prevent the delivery of food and other resources on which the Athenians depended for survival. Phocion knew that for nearly a decade after Athens's surrender the city had been exposed to what amounted to strangulation by any invading force that could occupy the now unwalled stretch of land between Piraeus and Athens. To make matters worse, he also learned that not just the Spartans but also some Athenians hostile to the democ-racy had celebrated the disappearance of these fortified safeguards. They praised the change as the "start of freedom for all of Greece," as the elitist Xenophon reported.[1]

Phocion also knew that after 403 the victorious Spartans had waged military campaigns of revenge to punish other enemies in mainland Greece and taken unprecedented steps in international re-lations. The new Spartan policy involved them with the superpower of the eastern Mediterranean region, the Persian Empire. The Greeks customarily expressed their awe of the power of the Persian monarch by referring to him simply as the Great King. With its capital situated in what is today Iran, the Persian state ruled enormous amounts of territory, from what is now Turkey to the borders of Pakistan and Afghanistan. This empire ruled countless diverse populations and controlled massive wealth. Its military strength could be overwhelming, so long as its royal family did not self-destruct in orgies of murderous conflict among relatives competing for the throne.

Many Greek city-states located in the westernmost regions of Persian territory where the continent of Asia met the Mediterranean Sea had long resisted Persian rule. When in the early fifth century BCE Greek city-states along the western coast of Turkey rebelled against Persian control, the Athenians sent a military force in support that ultimately failed in its mission. The damage done by this expedition, however, enraged Darius I, the Great King. In revenge, he and his successor Xerxes launched what are known as the Persian Wars, a series of invasions of mainland Greece between 490 and 479 that at one point destroyed Athens's urban center. But Phocion would have been specifically encouraged to take to heart from the Athenians' most treasured memory of this period: their leading role in eventually repulsing these unprecedented attacks. It had astonished the Greek world — including the Athenians themelves — that they and their allies had together driven out this leviathan of a foreign enemy. The Athenians also remembered that the invading Persians had been aided by some Greeks, including the Thebans, Athens's nearby neighbors to the north.

Phocion's next history lesson would have emphasized the boundless ambitions of Athens's most detested enemy, the Spartans. The Spartans set themselves apart from most other Greeks by living as an oligarchy that strictly regulated citizens' lives, from education to sex, and barred commerce, money, and immigrants. They also notoriously enslaved neighboring Greeks to be the workers who provided Spartan citizens with food, supplies, and services. They called these formerly free Greeks *helots* (the captured). Adult male helots had to be servants for Sparta's hoplites while on campaign and also themselves fight in battles against Sparta's enemies. Sparta's male citizens spent their time in military training and social gatherings designed to reinforce their infamously idiosyncratic mode of life. Spartans recognized two royal families, whose eldest males, Sparta's joint kings, commanded their military expeditions.

Following the Peloponnesian War, the Spartans decided to establish their reputation as the most powerful Greek state east of southern Italy and Sicily. They accordingly sent military support to Greeks who were rebelling against Persia in Asia Minor. In 397, the current Great King, Artaxerxes II, responded by assembling a fleet to confront the Spartans there, whom he labeled the most shameless of men. He hated the Spartans especially because they had supported his younger brother, Cyrus, in a recent civil war to determine who would replace their father as king.

The Spartans appointed Agesilaus, one of their kings and their leading military commander, to head their strike against the Persians. Agesilaus dramatically demonstrated the epochal significance the Spartans bestowed on what they saw as their expedition to defend Greek freedom from barbarians when he kicked off his fleet's voyage east with a sacrifice on the island of Euboea close to the Athenian coast. With this ceremony, he was specifically recalling Agamemnon, the leader of the Greeks in the Trojan War famous from Homer's *Iliad* and Aeschylus's tragedy *Agamemnon*. Agamemnon had made his own daughter Iphigenia a human sacrifice at the same spot on Euboea to try to win divine favor for his army's campaign against Troy. Agesilaus's sacrifice weirdly invoked an ill-starred precedent, for Agamemnon had turned out to be a disastrous commander, the war against Troy dragged on for ten dismal years, and on his long-delayed return to Greece Agamemnon was murdered by his wife. This omen proved accurate: the Spartans failed in their high ambitions for international dominance.

First the Boeotians from the Greek mainland led by Thebes disrupted Agesilaus's sacrificial ceremony to signal their rejection of Sparta's pretensions to the leadership of the Greeks. And then when Agesilaus did get his force to Asia Minor, prideful rivalries among Spartan leaders for preeminence and the inherent difficulty of this overseas mission prevented any quick outcome to the war. Meanwhile, the Athenians waged a civil war that enabled them to rid themselves of the Spartan-supported regime of the Thirty Tyrants. With democracy established, they made a startling decision to ensure their safety: they asked for financial assistance from their ancestral enemy the Persian king! Their goal was to use Persian money to rebuild their military strength against their enemies at home, meaning above all the Spartans. So intense were the anti-Spartan feelings among the majority of Athenian voters that they also authorized an alliance with their former Greek enemies Thebes, Corinth, and Argos (the latter two located in the northeast Peloponnese).

This shocking reversal in Athens's traditional foreign policy had paid dividends by the winter of 396/5. At that point, Artaxerxes II began sending funds to mainland Greek states willing to combat Sparta's aggressive dominance over them. Learning about these precedent-shattering events must have deepened Phocion's growing awareness that persistent ambiguity characterized human life. International relations conducted by a direct democracy controlled by the many obviously could take abrupt changes of direction.

The friction generated by the shifting allegiances among the Greek city-states soon led to a drawn-out conflict known as the Corinthian War (395–387), so named because the anti-Spartan Greek allies installed their war council in the city-state of Corinth, where much of the land fighting occurred. The geographical location of Corinth on the narrow isthmus connecting the Peloponnese peninsula to mainland Greece offered central access by land and sea for delegates to attend strategy meetings. Alarmed by this unanticipated threat, the Spartans recalled Agesilaus from Asia Minor while dispatching other prominent commanders to attack Thebes. Those generals fell miserably short in their campaign, however, one dying in the field and the other disgraced and exiled for his failure. Sparta's forces did win two land battles against Greek foes, but these victories were not enough to undo the anti-Spartan alliance.

In 394, when Phocion was about eight, he probably heard that the Athenian naval commander Conon had teamed up with the Persian fleet that had helped turn things in a better direction for the Athenians. Conon won a victory over a Spartan-led armada off Cnidos on the southern coast of Asia Minor. This hard-fought encounter so seriously weakened Sparta's naval resources that the Athenian commander and his Persian counterpart were able to sail back to Athens together. There they oversaw the reconstruction of the fortifications of the port of Piraeus. It was as if the vulnerable throat of the Athenians had once again donned armor to protect it from strangulation. Now the people could again be confident of importing the resources they needed to live and exporting the goods whose sale brought them income. In analyzing Phocion's later policy recommendations for Athens, it is key to recognize that he could not have missed the significance of Athens's regaining its safety because of cooperation with a powerful foreign monarchy.

The Corinthian War in the late 390s descended into a tense stalemate in which neither Greek side could succeed without support from Persia. The Spartans opened contacts with the Great King's representatives and simultaneously hosted a delegation of Athenians to discuss peace. The tentative agreement reached at Sparta satisfied no one. Artaxerxes II rejected it out of hand, and the Athenian Assembly exiled its representatives for failing to insist on the freedom of the Greeks in Asia Minor as a prerequisite for a treaty. Their fate could have been worse. A century earlier, when at the time of the Persian Wars the Athenian Lycidas had proposed to the Council of Five Hundred that it explore accommodation with the Persian king instead of going to war, his fellow citizens spontaneously stoned him to death as a traitor. And when the women of Athens heard of his proposal, they rushed to his home and stoned his wife and children as well. So Phocion as a youngster had already learned vividly both from history and also from present circumstances how dire the punishment could be for Athenians who attempted to serve their polis in crucial situations but then disappointed the expectations of the voters.

The majority of Athenians at this time clearly longed for their now-past glory days of the mid-fifth century, when they determined their future entirely on their own. But their only current option was to find some route to safety in a world dominated by a foreign king. How difficult this would be was shown by the failure of peace negotiations at Sparta that fueled a resumption of battles between Athens and Sparta. When Iphicrates' military innovations with light infantry and mercenaries put a scare into the Spartans, they, too, aggressively sought Persian support. This about-face in relations with their world's superpower proved successful. Phocion, like all Athenians, was horrified when the Spartans conducted a raid on Piraeus and seized control of the Hellespont, the narrow channel of sea connecting the northeastern Mediterranean with the Sea of Marmara on the route to the Black Sea.

This latter news was especially harrowing to Athenians because the Hellespont was the chokepoint for shipments of grain being transported by cargo ships from the fertile northern shores of the Black Sea (where in Ukraine a major supply of wheat for today's world is still grown). The Hellespont was, to extend the metaphor, the foreign throat of the Athenians. Most of their desperately needed food supplies reached them as cargoes transported through that narrow channel. Disastrously, however, Athens's naval commanders in the Hellespont region had now inexplicably ignored warnings that Sparta was going to launch an attack on this critical strait. Their failure gave the Spartans the power to choke Athens off despite the reconstruction of the Long Walls.

Reduced to desperation, in 386 the Athenians and the other mainland Greek states had to knuckle under to a Spartan initiative to arrange a treaty under the auspices of the Persian king Artaxerxes II. Phocion was at that date about fifteen and therefore aware of these seismic events affecting Athens. The terms of the so-called King's Peace were shocking. The Great King specified that the cities in Asia Minor and on the Mediterranean islands of Clazomenae and Cyprus would belong to him, the other Greek city-states would govern themselves, and the Greeks would observe a shared peace. Any Greek city-states that disobeyed would be punished by his armed forces. The king dismayed the Athenians by making Sparta his agent in Greece to oversee these arrangements. Phocion was old enough to realize that his home's long-cherished pride in its independence and power was now only a memory. He and his Athenian contemporaries found themselves in a new, harsher world, in which Sparta gloried in its status as a foreign potentate's watchdog over their ultimate fate.

Phocion was more than old enough to be paying attention to his city-state's uncertain position when in 380 the well-known Athenian speechwriter and teacher of rhetoric Isocrates (436–338) presented a radical solution to Athens's danger. Isocrates customarily refrained from addressing the Assembly, claiming he could not speak loudly enough to be understood there. Instead, he expressed his controversial political advice in writings, which he wanted people to discuss. On this occasion, he argued that Athens could improve its international situation only if his countrymen came to terms with their Greek enemies. Then, he said, it would be feasible "for us to try as hard as possible to transfer the war here in Greece over to Asia as fast we can." This farfetched plea for a Panhellenic crusade against the Persian Empire as a strategy to unite the bitterly divided mainland Greek communities came to nothing. Nevertheless, Isocrates' words testified to the depth of the distress permeating his homeland. A politically inclined young Athenian in his early twenties like Phocion would have comprehended this anxiety all too well.[2]

Characteristically, the Spartans soon proceeded to foul their own nest by violently bullying their fellow Greeks. By 379 the Thebans were so incensed at this behavior that they expelled the garrison that the Spartans had forced upon them in 382. In 378 the Spartans in retaliation sent one of their current kings, Cleombrotus I, followed by a large force commanded by Agesilaus, to invade Theban territory. The Athenians responded by dispatching a mercenary contingent commanded by Chabrias, Phocion's friend at Plato's Academy. Chabrias, some fifteen to twenty years older than Phocion and therefore eligible for positions of high responsibility in Athens's defense, became the most important influence on Phocion in the latter's early military career. Since Phocion was now old enough to serve in the infantry, it is possible that he was included in Chabrias's expedition as a hoplite or a cavalryman. His relationship with Chabrias would have made him eager to join the older general against the Spartans threatening Thebes.

Chabrias was known for military daring and invention. A decade earlier, for example, he had made a secret nighttime landing with his troops on the island of Aegina off the western shore of Attica. He then set a trap for a Spartan garrison that was stationed there to threaten raids against Athens. His surprise worked; the Spartans fell for his deception and were forced to flee the island. This time, to defeat Thebes Chabrias devised an even more striking tactic. To face Agesilaus's invasion force, he took his men to a hilltop outside the city. There they formed a defensive position alongside Theban troops. The Spartans began their attack by sending light-armed soldiers wielding javelins up the hill; the ascent was challengingly steep for hoplites weighed down by their heavy metal outfits and weapons. When Chabrias's force blocked this initial attack, Agesilaus ordered his heavy infantry to start laboring up the slope.

At this decisive moment, Chabrias commanded all his hoplites and the Theban cohorts to line up at the top of the hill — and to stand there at ease. That is, he told the infantrymen to rest their massive shields on the ground propped against their left knees and stand their spears up with their ends on the ground. This startling sight immediately froze Agesilaus. He had to wonder what his enemy could be doing. Surely, he concluded, they must have some awful surprise in store; this could not be simply a gesture of contempt for the Spartans. They must have something more in mind. But what was it? Perplexed, Agesilaus withdrew his men. The city of Thebes was saved, though the Spartans could still damage the surrounding countryside in revenge.

This incident became so famous among Greeks far and wide that the Athenians voted to honor Chabrias by erecting a statue of him in the Agora. He had it sculpted to show himself resolute in the at-ease posture that had baffled Sparta's most distinguished general of the age. Given what we hear about Phocion's strict modesty in his public life, he may have had reservations about this unmistakable boast by Chabrias. At the same time, Phocion learned once again a version of the lesson emphasized by Plato in his discourses and reinforced by Phocion's everyday existence in a fraught public life: there was a frequent disjunction between surface appearances and underlying reality. No one could have anticipated that the legendarily ferocious Spartans would turn and run from opponents ostentatiously lowering their weapons in the heat of battle.

Phocion saw the tangled history of Athenian-Spartan-Theban relations take yet another strange twist when not long afterward, in 378, a different Spartan commander conducted a surprise raid into Athenian territory. The Athenians protested in vain to the Spartans about this infringement of the shared peace. Responding to Sparta's arrogant disregard for the treaty, Phocion's countrymen now contracted an alliance with their ancient and bitter enemy, Thebes. This unprecedented swerve in Athenian foreign policy starkly underlined how fungible interstate relations had become in Greece. Phocion certainly would keep this point in mind in future years when he had to participate in wrenching decisions concerning how far Athens should go in restricting its treasured independence by making deals with other states.

At this point in the early 370s, the Athenians continued their drive for an effective defense against Spartan attacks and the revival of their past military strength. With the Persian king slow to respond to affairs so far away, they began extending their alliances with Greeks to the east. This new policy culminated in 378/7 with the announcement of a new league of allies, the Second Athenian League, that with its sixty-some members was reminiscent in its size of the Delian League, the alliance established by Athens in the fifth century following the Persian Wars. That earlier confederacy had become notorious for Athens's increasing dominance over its nominally free Greek allies and the extortion of financial dues. The

Spartans had exploited these coercive developments to rally opposition against Athens, which culminated in the outbreak of the Peloponnesian War. Conscious of the need to forge a new paradigm of international alliance, the Athenians now proclaimed in an inscription on public display that their goal was to cooperate with their allies "so that the Spartans will permit the Greeks, free and autonomous, to live in peace, possessing with security the territory that is their own." The allies were guaranteed any government they chose, garrisons were imposed, and financial payments for operating expenses were regarded as contributions, not compulsory dues.[3]

To emphasize the new league's difference from the Delian League, the Second Athenian League put its finances under the control of a joint council of the allies instead of Athens alone. No required amount of contributions was to be levied. Most of the sixty or so members of the league were island city-states, but Thebes also joined. Sparta responded to the threat to its power by dispatching yet another expedition against Thebes, but this one, too, came up short when Agesilaus fell seriously ill. The danger to Athens continued, however, especially as a result of the Spartans' move to cut their enemy's food supply chain by mobilizing their warships to block grain-carrying merchant ships' access to Piraeus. This naval blockade precipitated a frightening crisis for all Athenians, military and civilian.

It is in this fraught situation for his homeland that Phocion in 376 makes his entry into the surviving historical record as the commander of a warship at the tender age of twenty-six. Chabrias had once again been voted into overall charge of the Athenian response to the threat posed by the Spartan fleet, and he characteristically devised an ingenious stratagem. Calculating that his warships had their best chance of defeating Sparta's force in a battle fought in the open sea, he lured the Spartan fleet away from its blockade by launching a siege of the city-state of Naxos, an island in the Aegean Sea southeast of Athens. His strategy worked. The Spartan commander sailed his ships to the island to rescue its inhabitants from an Athenian takeover. This confrontation set the stage for Phocion to become a military hero.

CHAPTER SEVEN

Winning Glory as a
Young Naval Commander

Phocion was holding the position of a trierarch commanding a warship for the usual term of a year when he sailed into battle at Naxos in 376 as part of the Athenian fleet led by Chabrias. By assuming this post, Phocion was fulfilling a liturgy (*leitourgia*, "obligatory public service"), as Greeks designated the heavy financial responsibilities required of citizens who were members of the Athenian elite. Liturgies were crucial to Athens's communal operations because the city-state levied no income tax per se. Other liturgies included helping pay for Athens's many religious festivals and public entertainments, including the tragedies and comedies that made Athenian culture famous. In return for providing these large sums, richer citizens earned public approval and respect, which could help fend off judicial attacks on their performance in office or their political stances. Serving as a trierarch therefore can be seen in modern terms as a form of annual tax on the rich to help provide for national defense; trierarch was not an elected office like that of strategos.

Phocion

About the time that Phocion was conducting his trierarchy, Athens initiated a procedure for richer Athenians to share the cost of this liturgy, but it is not recorded whether any other well-off men helped him raise the equivalent of the approximately fifteen years' wages for a worker that a trierarch had to spend of his own money to complete his liturgy. In addition to this large personal expenditure, Phocion's service as a trierarch required him to go to great lengths to make his warship operational. He faced multiple practical hurdles as a commander in a citizen militia force. Athens's original plan for manning the navy, at least according to the traditional history of their distant past that its citizens heard, had been to rely on conscription. But over time it had become clear that this system was insufficient. Conscripts could turn out to be physically unfit, or they could simply disappear, with no feasible way for the state to locate them. Athens had no police force to track down deserters. As a result, the responsibility for assembling and maintaining a functional crew had become one of the responsibilities of trierarchs.

Phocion therefore faced the challenge of recruiting the 170 men who would row his ship as part of the approximately 200-man crew of a trireme. At the beginning of announced naval campaigns, rowers assembled in the main port of Athens. That year's trierarchs would then compete with one another to enlist the best candidates. As trierarch, Phocion had to offer a financial bonus to collect enough men to agree to row his warship, supplementing their state pay out of his own resources to motivate them to exert themselves while on duty. The shortage of men able and willing to do the exhausting and dangerous job of rowing triremes generated ongoing problems for richer citizens of Phocion's time who had been directed by the voters to conduct large-scale naval operations. For example, in 373 the general Timotheus enrolled everyone he could from the Piraeus crowd but still found his fleet more than ten thousand men short. He then had to sail throughout the islands of the Aegean Sea seeking non-Athenian rowers for hire.

It seems almost incredible that anyone, Athenian or not, agreed to serve as a rower on a trireme because the job was extraordinarily uncomfortable and stressful — indeed, downright terrifying. There was no escape from the intense sense of dread the rowers had to deal with in order to keep propelling their oars. Since they were seated facing rearward in three rows, one atop another, down in the belly of the ship, they could not see what was going on in the heat of battle. They knew that the enemy ship's ram could punch a hole in their hull at any moment, crushing those in its direct path and drowning many others before they could scramble up to the main deck. And even if they escaped drowning, once on deck the unarmed rowers faced javelin fire from marines positioned on the enemy ship. If the crew members surrendered before being killed, they faced a future of cruel enslavement.

Even the time that trireme rowers spent before and after the battle was physically trying in the extreme. These specialized vessels had narrow, unstable hulls built for speed, not comfort. Rowers had almost no room in which to store water or food, and no facilities for resting, urinating, or defecating. As a result, the rowers' bench was always uncomfortable and often filthy. In the heat of battle, feelings of extreme stress could suddenly empty the bowels of frightened rowers onto their comrades below and beside them.

Phocion as trierarch therefore faced formidable challenges in keeping his men focused on their mission and in optimum physical shape. Above all, he had to train his crew to follow orders so they could complete the complex maneuvers required of their trireme during the heat and terror of combat at sea. The crew had to propel their waterborne missile forward as fast as possible in order to rush through the line of the enemy's ships and shear off their enemy's oars. After the initial attack, they had to make fast turns to reverse course. Finally, they had to steel themselves for the perilous impact of ramming an enemy ship and then backing away quickly from the crash to preserve their own vessel's mobility. To raise his rowers' spirits and keep their bodies toned for these terrifying moments, Phocion might well have followed the example of Iphicrates, lining up his ship next to other triremes offshore and then staging a race to the beach.

Phocion also had to hire his other crew members, including a helmsman — a specialist who knew how to steer a warship in battle — and various support personnel. In addition he needed about ten armed marines to hurl missiles at enemy ships and, when possible, board them to kill their defenders, enslave their crews, and capture the valuable hull. Phocion's most crucial need was to secure a highly experienced navigator for his trireme. This specialist had to possess detailed knowledge of the islands, coasts, and prevailing currents and winds of the eastern Mediterranean where the fleet would operate. Phocion would have had to offer a substantial monetary bonus to win the best available candidate.

Logistics also posed a high hurdle for trierarchs. Phocion needed to bring his warship to land every day to allow the men to shop for provisions, make their own meals, collect drinking water, and catch an afternoon nap or a night's sleep outside on the ground. It was crucial for him to discover ahead of time suitable locations for these landings; they had to be places where the locals would set up markets for his crew to purchase necessities. Since maps in Phocion's time were rudimentary, he had to develop his own network of contacts to enable him to decide ahead of time where the crew could be satisfactorily accommodated. He also had to verify that his navigator knew enough marine geography to guide the ship over the open sea to these provisioning spots. When the navy's ships were sailing as a sizable fleet, that meant identifying places that could serve customers numbering in the many thousands. Finally, Phocion had to be constantly aware of the state of the equipment required to keep his ship operational, from sails to ropes to rudders and much more.

Above all, Phocion had to work to maintain the morale and loyalty of his crew. Many of the rowers were not Athenian citizens and therefore did not have an inherited loyalty to the community that might encourage them to persist through these extreme hardships and dangers. Their commander had to imbue them with that dedication. Even among the Athenians, as Demosthenes once remarked, there could be "a huge amount of desertion" of rowers if their trierarch did not provide them with enough additional money to pay their families' expenses. It was no secret, then, that successful leadership as a trierarch meant surmounting formidable psychological as well as practical challenges.[1]

As trierarch, Phocion had to show the Athenians in his crew that he respected them because he and they had the same citizenship status—they were not members of a professional military in the modern sense, or elected officials. In addition, naval commanders could be punished by the Assembly if citizen crewmembers lodged serious complaints. At the same time, Phocion had to find ways to institute a successful command hierarchy so that his frequently contentious fellow citizens would respect his orders, especially in life-threatening situations that offered no time for debate about who should do what, when. To earn the respect of his crew, he had to lead from the front by commanding his ship while exposed to enemy fire on the open deck. He needed to put himself at a clear risk of death to match the danger to his rowers sweating away below in their blind confinement, who lacked even a glimpse of how close they were to disaster from moment to moment.

Phocion's role in the ferocious action of the battle off Naxos in 376 against the Spartan fleet proved that he had what it took to excel as a trierarch. Chabrias had tried to confuse the enemy about the identity of the Athenian fleet by having all his force's ships lower their banners, but on this occasion the Spartan admiral arranged his fleet effectively. When the opposing fleets rowed into position, the Spartans overwhelmed the Athenian contingent at one end of the battle line. This initial success put the entire Athenian force in grave danger. If the Spartan ships that had punched through the Athenian lineup facing them could now swivel to attack the remaining Athenian triremes from the rear, all would be lost for Chabrias's fleet.

Phocion thereupon took the initiative on his own, for there was no reliable way for ship commanders to communicate with one another once battle was under way. He spurred a fast advance on the Spartans who were opposite him. The risk was high, and the fighting fierce. A terrific din erupted as ships crashed into one another, splintering oars, rudders, and hulls. Crews screamed to rally their martial spirit and in reaction to the painful, even deadly, injuries inflicted by the collisions of sea battles.

It was up to the trierarchs to keep their men literally and figuratively on course during this furor of blood and gore. In the melee of stress and uncertainty, Phocion's bold gamble succeeded. The Athenians' fleet rallied to gain its first victory in decades. (The last time the Athenians had prevailed in a naval battle had been in the Peloponnesian War.) Phocion emerged as the hero of the Battle of Naxos. Its outcome raised his profile greatly because the Spartan threat to Athens's food supply chain had now been neutralized, ensuring the survival of Attica's inhabitants. This decisive win proved key in energizing the Athenians to continue to rebuild their navy, a goal they accomplished so successfully that in time they reduced Spartan power at sea to second-rate status.

The immediate follow-up to the Battle of Naxos also enhanced Phocion's reputation. Maintaining Athens's national naval power depended on a steady, large supply of money to finance the construction and maintenance of warships and to pay tens of thousands of crew members. In the glow of victory Chabrias decided to send out a mission to raise money from the members of the Second Athenian League. This was a potentially divisive move. As mentioned earlier, during its heyday of hegemony in the mid-fifth century, Athens had abused its leadership of the Delian League's navy by enforcing demands for high dues. The memory of the First Athenian League's oppression had made financing the fleet of the recently formed Second Athenian League a sensitive issue. Since even after the Naxos victory Athens lacked the strength to compel payments from unwilling allies, any effort to revive the brute-force compulsion for payments that had corrupted the Delian League was sure to destroy the alliance. This, in turn, would gravely undermine Athens's safety in the face of continued Spartan hostility. By the league's regulations, financial contributions were completely voluntary. Collecting money from the allies was therefore a job calling for a high level of diplomacy and persuasion.

Chabrias as overall commander initially designated Phocion to take twenty triremes to help him collect the allies' payments. Evidently, Chabrias believed that this show of force was needed to frighten the allies into satisfying their financial obligations to the league. Phocion, however, told his superior that sending this number of triremes was appropriate only if the intention was to make war on the allies. He had realized that Chabrias was trying to use intimidation to raise the money, an aggressive tactic that would surely sabotage the mission. Perhaps Phocion was remembering the history of the renowned fifth-century Athenian hero Themistocles, who had ingeniously figured out a strategy to defeat the enemy in the most crucial naval battle of the Persian Wars, but then disgraced himself by using Athenian warships to extort money from other Greeks. Phocion told Chabrias that he could do the job using only one ship, his own. Startlingly, Chabrias agreed to let him do just that, even though Phocion was still too young by Athenian standards for such a key task. Chabrias's confidence in his young officer proved well founded: Phocion returned from his visits to the allies with numerous supply ships filled with many thousands of silver coins (no paper money existed), enough to meet the allies' financial responsibilities to the alliance.

Phocion had performed with flying colors. He had succeeded so spectacularly at collecting the funds because he had made sure to hold discussions in the allied cities about their concerns, dealing respectfully and honestly with their public officials while avoiding threats of violence. That is, he behaved like a mature adult deeply considerate of the practical circumstances of the various Greek communities. He had grasped the necessity of using persuasion to secure the allies' aid and avoid offense to their notions of pride and self-worth. In short, he apparently recognized the overriding power of emotions in human interactions and went to great lengths to prevent crises provoked by arrogance, condescension, or hurt feelings. He deftly convinced the allies that he was like them, creating what in modern psychological theory can be called homophily — a feeling of bonding among people who come to regard others as similar to them. His technique on this crucial mission to the non-Athenian allies is worth remembering for its contrast with his customarily confrontational style of dealing with his fellow citizens at home.

To grasp the kudos that Phocion garnered at Athens from his

impeccably honorable conduct with the allies, we need to recognize that Athenian naval commanders might behave very differently. In fact, they could act as pirates, exploiting official Athenian warships. Demosthenes, for example, accused trierarchs of raising money for their expeditions by launching private plundering missions they called favors (that is, "protection" for maritime merchants) and by exercising outright extortion. This money could easily find its way into the commanders' own private purses. The orator Lysias blasted one Diotimus for having pocketed the enormous sum of forty talents (a talent was the rough equivalent of twenty years' wages for an average working man) in the early 380s by forcing merchant ship owners and import-export traders to cough up protection money; Diotimus indignantly claimed he was being slandered.[2]

Some decades later, in the mid-350s, similar accusations were made that Athenian representatives sailing to Asia Minor on an official diplomatic mission had conspired with the ship's commander to attack a merchant ship. They stole an unimaginable sum from its cargo — this time the equivalent of what a well-paid worker would earn in about 150 years. They retained the money for themselves instead of turning it in to the public treasury as legitimate booty captured from an enemy. On another occasion, an Athenian commander was accused of malfeasance that avoided violence but subverted public policy. He used his warship to bring home to Athens vine props, cattle, framed doors, and timber from a neighboring island, all for his own personal benefit.

Even this diversity of examples does not cover all the cases of the private misuses of triremes. Some Athenians would even purchase a functional warship for their own use. As hard as it seems to imagine, they could buy, equip, and hire a crew to operate a top-of-the-line battleship. One such wealthy Athenian around the 380s, Makartatos, bought a trireme and sailed it, fully crewed, to the island of Crete, where he used it for raiding. So politically sensitive were his targets that his private mission was discussed in the Assembly as likely to shatter the current state of peace between Athens and Sparta.

These outrageous abuses of power reflected not only commanders' selfish desires to enrich themselves, but also the problems that had begun to plague Athens's arrangements for public financing of the navy that played so essential a role in the city-state's national defense. In Phocion's time, trierarchs at the end of their year in office more and more frequently failed to return to state control the ship's equipment that was given to them when they took up their commands. Instead, they retained these valuable tools for their own use. Preserved records show, for instance, that in 357/6 up to a fourth of Athens's warships could not be readied for use because they did not have the necessary equipment to prepare them for active service. Some trireme commanders failed to return this equipment for years and years, and as a result they might eventually be declared public debtors. A court case from this period concerns a trierarch who was accused of owing equipment to the state that he refused to turn in for years. At this same point in the mid-fourth century, Athens began conscripting rowers to ensure a full supply of the manpower needed to preserve the city-state's safety.

Phocion as a politically active adult certainly recognized that there were complex reasons for the remarkable failure of Athens's formal administrative structure to keep its navy properly equipped. Some motivations were well intentioned. Men responsible for fulfilling a trierarch liturgy could decide that private arrangements were more reliable than public procedures for obtaining the equipment on time. So some of these trierarchs held on to the equipment they were originally allotted, intending to use it again the next time they were liable for the liturgy and had to prepare a trireme for service. Citizens who were not currently serving as trierarchs could also loan or lease to current trierarchs the ship's equipment they had themselves previ-ously privately purchased from the craftsmen who had manufactured it. On occasion, these entrepreneurs could even hold on to the equip-ment for decades to maintain their improper source of income. The more patriotic of these former trierarchs, those who were not simply corrupt, apparently believed that their private initiative in making trireme equipment available at a price was the best way to ensure that the national fleet would be ready to sail into battle when needed. It was too risky to expect that government procedures would be rig-orously followed. They wanted to make sure that sufficient mate-rials were kept in public storage to supply all Athens's warships.

Scholars today disagree about whether the semi-privatization of the administration and use of Athens's fleet weakened the overall military competence of the city-state in the crucial international theater of naval warfare while also damaging the income stream of the state. One view is that untrustworthy citizens and tax dodgers were undermining the prospects of Athenian democracy to remain strong enough to defend its independence and maintain its finan-cial health. A competing interpretation is that these changes in fact amounted to an engine helping to propel the Athenian economy and enhancing the city-state's prospects for keeping the government truly democratic. Whatever the forces behind the new directions in public interest and private self-enrichment, Phocion from the start of his prolonged career in public service found himself im-mersed in a divided, disputatious, and insecure democracy. Its domestic and international politics were for all practical purposes constantly in turmoil because neither the elite nor the poor citizens could be unilaterally trusted to fulfill their civic duties.[3]

All this is not to say that the Athenian government simply gave up trying to regulate naval operations for its citizens' shared ad-vantage and benefit. The officials in charge of the administration of the organization and finances of the national fleet had to submit extensive annual records, which were made public via inscriptions. And they had a lot to manage in Phocion's time. Following their victory in the Peloponnesian War in 404, the Spartans had forced the Athenians to reduce their formerly huge fleet to only 12 naval ships. In the fourth century, however, that number recovered exponentially over time. In 387, the navy had expanded to around 70 ships. Ten years later, there were 100 triremes. By 325, the navy had soared to 417 ships, counting warships of all sizes.

Keeping track of the navy's accounts was an exercise in open government presided over by the Council of Five Hundred, and the details were available to everyone. Archaeologists have found remains of a publicly displayed stone inscription, for example, that was six feet tall and three feet wide and had some five thousand entries inscribed on it of the naval administrators' accounts and inventories for the year 357/6.[4] The Athenian government worked to keep the money flowing to pay for all this activity. In addition to devising ways to persuade citizens to share the financial burden of large-scale liturgies in general, significantly increased taxes on wealthier citizens were also imposed in the third quarter of the fourth century. These levies financed enormous expansion of the infrastructure and the buildings in the three naval ports in Piraeus that served for building, repairing, and storing equipment for the Athenian navy.

In the environment of uncertainty enveloping Athens's system of national defense, a trierarch who succeeded to the degree that Phocion did was certainly going to be lauded as an outstanding citizen. But that was not all that would have distinguished the young Phocion in the eyes of his fellow citizens. He also exerted a remarkable influence on his older mentor Chabrias during wartime. Chabrias could be lethargic at times but then tended to catch fire. He was sometimes so full of fury that he rushed into dangerous wartime situations without thinking them through. This rashness seriously elevated the peril to the Athenians he was leading into battle. In fact, Chabrias ultimately threw away his own life trying to force a landing when his flagship hurried ahead of the rest of his fleet during a battle of the Social War (discussed below). Phocion did not accompany him on that engagement. When Phocion was present with Chabrias, the young man was somehow able to marshal the diplomacy and persuasive techniques needed to guide his distinguished if unpredictable older mentor. Chabrias then made sounder decisions because Phocion showed himself able to be simultaneously both "safe and action-filled," as Plutarch puts it.[5]

There were lasting ramifications for Phocion from his role in the victory at Naxos and its highly beneficial consequences for Athens. The celebrated triumph in this battle took place in the middle of the late summer month of Boedromion, the time of year during which the Athenians held their internationally renowned annual ceremony celebrating their worship of the divine Demeter and Persephone at Eleusis, just west of Athens. This sacred ritual, known as the Great Mysteries, was especially significant because it promised a happy afterlife to initiates. Chabrias commemorated his fleet's incredible success by every year paying for wine to supply the crowds who attended this prominent festival. His munificent gifts contributed to preserving not only his own memory but also the reputation of Phocion. The young hero was remembered as an insightful commander whose astute decision to take such daring action at a crucial moment had saved the day for his homeland.

Phocion as a trierarch enjoyed a spectacular start to his public career even before he turned thirty, the age at which Athenians thought men reached their full capabilities to promote the shared advantage and benefit of all. Phocion's remarkable success at this stage of his life gave him the kind of highly positive reputation for valuable public service that helped promote his unprecedented success in being elected strategos, Athens's highest office, over the course of some five decades. His early life history makes it all the more striking that his life would end in a fatal downfall engendered by the hatred of the majority of the community to which he officially belonged and to which he had devoted his career. Luck (*Tyche*) was a divinity in Greek thought and seen as notoriously unpredictable and incomprehensible in its motivations. Certainly some bad luck in Athens's international relations contributed to Phocion's fall from grace, but as we will see his own decisions played a decisive role in his fate.

We have seen that Phocion was often brash and even directly offensive to other citizens in his public remarks. But we have to remember that Phocion was elected general more times than any other Athenian in history. Moreover, as we will also see, he was chosen to serve on ambassadorial missions to negotiate with foreign powers at crucial junctures. These contradictions show up throughout his long life. As noted before, it seems that he somehow managed to be more cordial and emotionally soothing toward foreigners than those with whom he was supposed to have developed a strong sense of belonging. One explanation might be that his attitudes toward "the many" of Athenian democracy were not fixed early in life but evolved until they finally reached a level of serious discomfort and disillusionment. After all, his mission to the allies following the Battle of Naxos shows that he could, when he wished, be marvelously effective both in motivating his fellow citizens who were doing the horrifying duty of manning triremes and also in dealing with foreigners over difficult matters involving controversial financial commitments. Phocion's choices about his conflicting behaviors impelled him to his triumphs but also to his ultimate tragedy.

CHAPTER EIGHT

Facing Midlife Challenges

O ur sources fall silent about Phocion's life and career over
the next fifteen or so years following his military and diplomatic success in 376. We do know that he was married twice and
had at least one daughter and a son named Phocus (the only one
of Phocion's wives or children whose name is preserved). In addition, the frequency of his election as one of the city-state's annual
generals means that he must have held office regularly during this
period. Given that Phocion was by Athenian standards of age still
a neophyte in his public career in the mid-370s, it makes sense to
surmise that he remained connected to Chabrias. In that case, he
would certainly have been involved in the continuing military and
diplomatic jockeying for power among Athens, Sparta, and Thebes.

War on land and sea among these three mainland Greek states
and their allies roared ahead after the Battle of Naxos, but none
achieved dominance. In 375 the combatants reluctantly renewed
their commitment to the King's Peace, but the Spartans soon broke
their promise to respect the independence of their rivals by launching new campaigns against other Greeks. The Athenians responded

as best they could. When a Spartan expedition gained control of the city-state of Corcyra in around 375 or 374, the Corcyrans appealed to the Athenians for help. The Assembly authorized Timotheus to prepare a fleet for their defense. Corcyra was located on the large island (today's Corfu) off the west coast of Greece that provided the most important stepping-stone for sea traffic to and from the prosperous Greek and non-Greek communities in southern Italy and Sicily. The Athenians feared the Spartans could gain a choke-hold on that crucial supply chain from the west. But Timotheus encountered great difficulty in finding enough rowers for his fleet's triremes and, as we have seen, had to scour the islands around Athens for more.

Enraged at Timotheus's delay, the Athenians deposed him from office in a trial for incompetence at which he escaped condemnation only through the intervention of influential foreign friends. Jason, the tyrant (sole ruler) of the Greek city-state of Pherae in central Greece, and Alcetus, king of Epirus in northwestern Greece, traveled to Athens to plead for his acquittal. Amyntas, king of Macedonia, to the north of Greece, shipped timber to Timotheus's house to show how much he valued their relationship; wood (pine and cedar) of sufficient strength and length for building Athens's warships had to be imported from northern forests because Attica had been deforested. Dismayed at this treatment by his fellow citizens and having bankrupted himself trying to hire trireme rowers, Timotheus left Athens. He took a lucrative job working as a commander of mercenaries serving the supremely rich Great King of Persia.

What happened to Timotheus reinforced for Phocion four concrete examples of the harsh realities of pursuing a career in high office in Athens. First, Athenians were merciless in punishing their officials for falling short of expectations. Second, the personal expenses that commanders were expected to undertake to fulfill their military duties could ruin their families. Third, service with the monarch of a superpower offered a way to relieve monetary pressures for those willing to travel far from home and operate in unfamiliar and dangerous environments. And finally, good relations with foreign leaders who wielded influence in Athens could be invaluable in protecting someone from the consequences of decisions made by his fellow citizens in anger.

Since Phocion had proven himself more than capable as a military leader, he must have participated on missions outside Attica — hostilities among the Greek states continued to boil at a high temperature. Perhaps he served as Chabrias's colleague when the older man in late 376 led a force to the northeast region of the Greek peninsula to help the people of Abdera resist an invasion by their neighbors from Thrace. This region was notorious for the fearsome groups of raiders it produced. Athens had a vested interest in keeping it from falling into the hands of non-allies because it played a key role in safeguarding open routes for supplies being imported from farther north and east. Phocion could also have been with Chabrias in 369 at Corinth on assignment to keep the isthmus out of enemy hands and therefore open for access to the Greek mainland and the Peloponnese peninsula.

Competent leaders were in demand to support Athens's safety against the continuing aggressions of Sparta and Thebes. The King's Peace more and more become just a shredded specter of its original charter, as evidenced by, among other acts, the Thebans' attacks on and annexation of important towns in their region. Perhaps the worst episode was their treatment of the nearby city-state of Plataea in 373. Plataea was ethnically Boeotian but the Plataeans had always refused to become part of a Boeotian federal alliance. The city-state had won everlasting fame for having been the only community in its region to stand with the Athenians against the Persians and their

Greek ally Thebes during the Persian Wars. The Plataeans' fate therefore became doubly tragic when their neighbors now expelled them, razed their city's buildings, and merged their land into Theban territory.

Isocrates wrote a speech that he put in the mouth of a fictional Plataean, whom he depicted as pleading with the Athenians to take action to aid these descendants of the soldiers who had fought so boldly for Greek freedom: "We are so far from being seen as deserving equality with all the other Greeks that even though we have kept the peace and there are treaties in force, we not only lack any share in the freedom that everyone else enjoys, we are not even judged worthy to exist in a condition of moderate slavery!" The tragedy of Plataea, a treasured ally of Athens, generated massive resentment against Thebes among the Athenians. They sheltered some refugees from the devastated city-state, but they did not vote to launch a rescue mission.[1]

Enmity between Thebes and Sparta as rivals for power in Greece grew even more acrid. The Spartans organized a large-scale invasion of Theban territory in 371, but they experienced a terrible defeat at Leuctra in which their commander Cleombrotus I, one of their dual kings, and a substantial number of their dwindling male population were killed. They had to make an ignominious retreat. The victory by the Thebans proved so crushing that observers attributed it to a divine force having lured the Spartans into a trap as retribution for betraying their oath to keep the peace in Greece. Further Athenian efforts to bring all the parties once again to the peace table ended in failure.

By 369, the stress among the competing Greek powers had grown to the point that Athens and Sparta did what seemed nearly unthinkable for these two traditionally irreconcilable enemies — they agreed to a formal alliance with each other against Thebes. They were not bashful about proclaiming their goal. Both the Spartans and the Athenians would exercise hegemony over Greece, the former by land and the latter by sea. With internecine battles among the Greeks nevertheless continuing, the Thebans in response in 367/6 sent an embassy to Artaxerxes II, the Great King. They asked him to intervene to revive the peace treaty originally concluded under his aegis. Most likely a ploy by the Thebans to secure their own superiority, this idea went nowhere back in Greece when the terms for the new treaty were delivered.

To show the Athenians how furious this stalemate made them, the Thebans used a dispute at Oropos as their excuse for invading and then capturing its territory in 366. This community lay along the border between Theban and Athenian territory. Like many borderlands, it had long been a focus of competition between the much larger powers on its margins. Thebes's intervention abolished the Athenians' influence in Oropos, enraging them. The Thebans and the Athenians were both obsessed with controlling Oropos because it housed the sanctuary and oracle of the legendary figure Amphiaraus, whose reputation as a seer and a warrior induced people to regard him after his death as able to predict the future as well as offer healing to his suppliants. The demand for access to his shrine rivaled that of the famed oracle of the god Apollo at Delphi. Archaeological excavation has revealed that large sums of money were spent to build more and better buildings at Oropos in the fourth century. These expenditures emphasize the sanctuary's continuing importance as a focus of international conflict.

Phocion was in his mid-thirties and basking in the glow of the reputation he had earned from his earlier military success when he became involved in the Oropos affair. He took part not as a military commander in the field, however, but as an Athenian citizen at home. Contrary to his usual preference, he decided to speak up in the Assembly. He was apparently motivated to address the situation not just as a matter of crucial foreign policy but also for personal reasons. Chabrias and Callistratus, another prominent political and military figure, were blamed for not having prevented the disaster at Oropos militarily and for then having agreed to arbitration with the Thebans. The Athenians put them both on trial on a charge of treason.

The height of bitterness this dispute reached among Athenians emerged dramatically in the meeting of the Assembly to decide what to do about the crisis. The heat of the public debate evidently provoked Phocion, who gave one of his rare public speeches, laying out the situation in detail. He addressed the Assembly's deeply divided audience on the subject of the conduct of the generals at Oropos, aiming to express his approval of their initiative to secure an arbitrated settlement rather than send their men into battle against the formidable victors of the Battle of Leuctra. Phocion advised Athens's voters to go to battle against the Thebans with their words, with which they were stronger, rather than with their weapons, with which they were weaker. Phocion's judgment that the Athenians in this case lacked the strength to get what they wanted enraged citizens holding the opposite view because he seemed to be insulting them by questioning their courage. His remarks opened him up to the same accusation of disloyalty to his homeland that had put Chabrias and Callistratus at risk of public execution.[2]

When the generals in the Oropos fiasco were put on trial, they were saved from condemnation on a very close vote through the support and speeches of prominent friends, including Plato, who made a rare appearance as a speaker, despite a threat from a political opponent, because, he said, it was "the proper thing to do for a friend." The speech to the jury by Callistratus was so powerfully moving that it inspired the young, indeed barely adult Demosthenes to aspire to a career in public speaking. Still, the commanders' acquittal did nothing to decrease the intensity of the blazing feelings of political hostility into which Phocion's pointed comments had inserted him. This incident presaged quite eerily the nature and the ferocity of subsequent political disagreements about Athenian international relations that would plague Phocion's later career and, indeed, provoke his eventual catastrophe.[3]

Perhaps the most important thing to note about Phocion's character at this point, nearly fifty years before his death, is that he seems never to have wavered from his belief that for national safety it was always necessary for the Athenians to be willing to negotiate with powerful opponents without setting conditions. He advised doing so even when it would exact a high price in terms of national pride and sense of autonomy. Moreover, he clearly believed that his belonging to his polis did not require him to tone down his ardor and directness in expressing his own views on policy. He was not deterred by other citizens fervently disagreeing with him.

The Athenians' psychological challenge in dealing with the reality of their diminished power lingered as internecine struggles continued among the states of Greece. The Thebans' aggressive successes motivated the Athenians to make the difficult decision to join the Spartans in opposing their northern neighbor. This conflict culminated in a climactic battle in 362 near the town of Mantinea in the central Peloponnese. Both sides intended this confrontation to decide once and for all which of the two rival alliances would dominate Greece. Whether Phocion served as an Athenian commander at Mantinea is unknown. As a prominent leader, however, he can hardly have avoided the implications of the stunning conclusion of this famous battle. The Thebans, led by their distinguished general Epaminondas, won the contest in the field by routing the Spartans and their allies, including Athens. But tragically for the Thebans, Epaminondas and Thebes's other leading commanders were killed. Exhausted by this struggle among themselves, the Greek states tried to create some kind of equilibrium by signing a treaty for a Common (Shared) Peace. But the Spartans refused to join. Consequently, instead of a new and stable balance of power in Greece, "greater uncertainty and tumult existed after the battle than had existed before it," as Xenophon glumly summed up the situation in the final words of his history of Greece.[4]

The next major issue in Athens's foreign policy for which we have evidence of Phocion's direct involvement indicates the desperate need of the Athenians to erase the humiliation they felt over the outcomes of the Oropos affair in 366 and the Battle of Mantinea in 362. Astonishingly, the now-weakened Athenians inserted themselves militarily into the affairs of the richest and most powerful state in their world, the Persian Empire. In the mid-360s, a widespread rebellion against the Great King had broken out among a number of his high-ranking subordinates who functioned as governors of the large provinces into which the Persian Empire was institutionally divided. Called satraps ("territory protectors"), these appointees of the monarch administered huge territories (satrapies) largely on their own. They were powerful figures because they commanded substantial military and financial resources.

In about 361, the Athenians voted to send commanders and troops to fight in Asia Minor on the western front of the Satraps' Revolt. This force was meant to aid the satraps rebelling against Artaxerxes II. The Athenians' motivation for their startling decision to confront the Great King is difficult to understand. They could not have had any reasonable expectation of being able to furnish enough additional military power to propel the rebellious Persian governors to victory over the Great King. And even if they had been successful, they had little to gain. There was no hope that Athenians could maintain a hold over Persian territory in Asia. There were also no obvious commercial advantages to be seized above and beyond the connections that already existed in international trade between Europe and Asia.

Most likely, the Assembly decided to join the Satraps' Revolt because the voters felt an overwhelming emotional need for revenge against the empire that more than a century earlier had attacked, sacked, and burned their city-state. There could also have been a financial motive. Warfare in ancient times always involved significant financial consequences for both sides. Losers could see their property destroyed, their valuables seized, their land taken over — their very bodies could be stolen from them when they were killed or sold as slaves. Winners could not only recoup their expenses but also profit from the depredations they imposed on those they conquered. And mercenaries could earn good salaries as well as get a share of the booty. The majority of Athenians may well have calculated that fighting in the Satraps' Revolt could bring them financial benefits from emoluments paid for joining the satraps' forces and from the sale of objects and persons plundered from the king's territory. If there was one thing that Greeks knew about the Persians, it was that the riches controlled by Persian satraps and the Great King were astronomical compared to their own.

This was certainly a fraught time for Athenian foreign policy. The Persian regime continued to try to extend its control over the Greeks wherever it could, for instance on the island of Samos in the mid-360s until the Athenians successfully intervened. As a result, a number of individual Greek commanders hired on as mercenaries in Persian service. Their motives were certainly monetary. Some of them accepted employment under the Great King, while others, such as King Agesilaus of Sparta, signed up to serve under a rebel satrap. Phocion decided to take a position in the latter category, as did his mentor Chabrias. It is not clear whether Phocion served as a mercenary commander personally hired by a satrap or had been dispatched as a general by the Athenian Assembly to help oppose Artaxerxes II's forces. It is attested, however, that around 361/0 he fought a battle in Asia Minor against Athenodorus, an Athenian who definitely was a mercenary commander working for the Great King against the satraps. The outcome of this clash was essentially a draw, presaging the looming end of the rebellion. Over time, the Satraps' Revolt lost its cohesion, leaving Artaxerxes still in power.

Regardless of whether Phocion fought in this foreign war as a private mercenary or on an official Athenian mission, he would have gained financially. His personal benefit may have been why he took the risk of signing up for this kind of dangerous work in distant lands, rather than his having acted with the expectation of making a difference in Athenian foreign policy. Phocion was descended from a well-off family, but his inherited wealth did not mean that he never encountered the kind of liquidity problems that often affected even well-off Greek families. Especially if a family's income depended primarily on farming or raising flocks, the income stream from its property could vary a great deal from time to time. Bad weather, crop and animal diseases, limited availability of tenants and workers, and capital investment needs could reduce the owner's revenue unpredictably. The resulting shortfall in ready money could last for quite some time if these harmful pressures were slow in dissipating. To continue to finance their customary lifestyle in the face of such setbacks, Athens's property owners often had to resort to borrowing money from private lenders. These sources usually charged high interest rates.

If Phocion did encounter money problems that induced him to serve as a mercenary, it was not the result of his spending habits. He was notorious for his frugality. Like Socrates, he went barefoot, in the manner of an ancient hunter-gatherer, except when weather conditions were extreme. He wore only an outer garment when he was out of the city or on a military campaign. Phocion's wife wore her husband's cloak instead of fine feminine clothes. She took along only a single slave to accompany her when she went out of the house — well-off matrons customarily had a group of servants follow them around everywhere. Phocion's bare-bones arrangements for himself and his spouse were conspicuous displays separating them from their well-off contemporaries. Phocion obviously did not feel a sense of belonging in terms of how he and his spouse should appear in public contexts.

His fellow Athenians found evidence for this attitude in Phocion's treatment of his son Phocus, for whose poorly documented existence our main source is Plutarch.[5] The chronology of Phocus's life is obscure, but at some point in his teenage years, perhaps in the late 350s, his father took the extraordinary step of packing him off to Sparta to experience its legendarily harsh and prolonged system of guidance for male youths. This highly regimented system for instilling proper values as defined by Spartan tradition stressed military skills, strict obedience, and painful punishments for perceived shortcomings. Sending Phocus to this distant boarding school meant Phocion had to come up with the considerable cash required to pay all the associated expenses.

He did just that, despite the hostile reaction to his decision expressed by other Athenians. They made plain their angry dismay at what they interpreted as Phocion's disdain for their customs as compared to those of their habitual enemies the Spartans. His detractors clearly believed that he was spending money to demonstrate his reluctance toward belonging to the wider Athenian community of the people. It seems likely that this negative conclusion endured, creating an impediment to Phocion's ability to convince other citizens that his policies were to the shared advantage and benefit of them all. This would matter a great deal when disputes later arose concerning how Athens should interact with foreign powers whom it could not defeat.

Phocion's controversial decision to pack his son off to Sparta apparently arose from the young man's public misbehavior, which embarrassed his father after the latter had spent the money to finance a special activity for Phocus marking out him as a member of the elite few. That is, Phocion paid for Phocus to train for performances as a rider vaulting on and off horses in competitions held as part of the annual Panathenaic festival in honor of the goddess Athena at Athens. This sort of rodeo sport was a very expensive pursuit: the participant (or his father) had to maintain a suitable horse, pay a trainer, and hold celebrations to mark victories in the contests. It turned out that it could also overinflate the ego of a self-centered boy who felt entitled. This syndrome afflicted the young Phocus. Elated by his costly success in public competitions, he began organizing party after party soaked with wine. Such conduct, our limited evidence reports, enraged his father; they never got along well afterward, so far as we can tell. We can, however, surmise that Phocus's ostentatiously self-indulgent lifestyle contributed to the view among Athenians that Phocion's family was setting itself apart from them.

A much more socially acceptable expenditure was Phocion's generosity in providing money to help less affluent families fund dowries for their daughters. Women of Phocion's social stratum were supposed to bring this endowment to their marriages as their own property, which supplemented their husbands' holdings. Since dowries were expected to be substantial, Phocion's charity could be costly. In fact, as mentioned above, one ancient report notes that Phocion's magnanimity and financial generosity to others in need were what earned him the official honorary designation Chrestos (Useful and Good).

Being a member of the Athenian elite did not guarantee financial liquidity, however. To repeat a salient fact of life at Athens, it was often the case that members of the social few found themselves property rich but cash poor. Reports whose details fit into the late 360s or 350s suggest that Phocion experienced situations in which his income fell short of his spending needs for reasons beyond his control. We saw this in his acceptance of mercenary service; another notable example of Phocion's at times possessing inadequate funds was his reaction when the Athenian Assembly decided to hold a large-scale sacrifice to the gods. Most likely, the voters authorized this particular costly expenditure because they feared that their city-state needed extra support from the divine to ward off some pressing danger. As was standard procedure when the city-state faced larger than usual expenses, the citizens officially voted for what they called contributions (*eisphorai,* "things carried in") to be made by Athens's richer citizens to provide the needed funds. These "donations" were in fact mandatory for all those who possessed the amount of property that made them liable for this de facto tax on the wealthy. Phocion was a member of this group and therefore one of the Athenians who was required to make such a gift. When he was approached to pay his share, however, he declined to provide the money. As officials continued to request his contribution, he finally responded in exasperation, "Ask those rich fellows over there! I would be disgraced if without paying back this man I gave you a contribution!" He was at the time pointing toward a moneylender standing nearby.[6]

Phocion must have been seriously overextended financially to make such a combative statement to the representatives of the people. He would not have casually acted against his consistent commitment to a career in public service as a prominent citizen. To avoid being punished legally for his refusal, he would have had to go to great lengths to prove that he was literally unable to furnish the amount due. He presumably did so. However, the difficulty in his nontechnological era of obtaining precise and convincing documentation of a person's wealth probably led other Athenians to remain skeptical of the truth of his assertion of financial difficulties. This controversial episode might have furnished yet another stimulus for his detractors to question the depth of his commitment to belonging to the Athenian polis. In a political context, the question of his veracity could even have been seen as indicating that Phocion's fidelity toward the people was less than unquestioned. In any case, the dispute seems to have been another prelude to the disastrous accusations of disloyalty that would be lodged against Phocion at the end of his life.

Archaeology provides an especially poignant piece of evidence for just how malevolent feelings became toward Phocion during his adult life. Curse tablets were small sheets of lead inscribed with the names of people whom the author of the tablet begged the gods to restrain or punish harshly. The sheets were deposited underground or posted in locations believed to attract divine attention. One curse tablet from probably the mid-fourth century lists the name Phocion along with other men and also two women, perhaps slaves of the men. Since some of the other men's names are of individuals attested as active in local politics, the Phocion on the tablet is most likely our protagonist. Specific details are unrecoverable, but the curse probably documents a bitter dispute over politics resulting in a court case. Given the widespread belief in the efficacy of curses, this document powerfully stresses how harsh some of the evaluations of Phocion the public figure had become as he grew older. [7]

CHAPTER NINE

Dealing with Macedon

The course of Athens's history in the mid-fourth century BCE further reveals why the issue of loyalty could have stirred up especially strong emotions against Phocion. As mentioned previously, Athens in the early 370s had once again become so ambitious that it had created the Second Athenian League to project its naval power into the eastern Mediterranean. The contributions the allies paid toward naval costs were crucial to maintaining Athens's financial stability. By the mid-fourth century, however, that income had been surpassed by the expenses the Athenians incurred during the never-ending hostilities against their Greek neighbors that continued after the inconclusive Battle of Mantinea in 362.

Other members of the league were feeling equally pinched by the time a non-Greek dynast named Mausolus, from Caria, on the southwest coast of Asia Minor, decided to take a hand in the affairs of important allies of Athens. He did so at the behest of the new Persian king, Artaxerxes III, his de facto overlord. Mausolus convinced Chios, Cos, and Rhodes, the most important island states off Asia Minor, to stop making their contributions to the league. He also persuaded Byzantium to join the revolt. The Byzantine city-state controlled the vital strait providing entrance and exit from the Sea of Marmara to the Black Sea along the Bosporus, a channel used by countless merchant ships, including those that brought grain to the port of Piraeus. Byzantium taxed that full stream of commercial traffic. By withdrawing from the Second Athenian League, the Byzantines could keep all the money they collected in tolls without sending any to help finance the league's navy.

The ensuing struggle between Athens and its disloyal (in Athenian eyes) allies is known as the Social War (357–355). When the ever-treacherous Thebans supported the rebel allies, the Athenians lost the war. Our sources fail to disclose whether Phocion took an active military role in this conflict, but it seems unlikely that as an experienced commander now in his mid-forties he would have remained uninvolved. This ill-fated conflict not only further weakened Athens; it also exacerbated the political split among citizens, who rushed to blame one another for their hard times. The divisive tone of a speech written by Isocrates known as the *Areopagiticus*, recalling the name of the council that originally had exercised special powers in Athenian democracy, exemplified the growing divide over which citizens should have the ultimate power of decision. The Athenians, Isocrates said, should revive the more class-structured original democracy of their ancestors because "they thought it was an error to judge useful and good citizens [i.e., the social elite] and wicked citizens [i.e., the people] as meriting the same influence; they privileged the type of equality that elevates and punishes citizens according to what they deserve. This is how our ancestors governed our polis — not by allowing anyone chosen by lottery to hold a political office but only the best citizens, the ones best equipped to do what was needed. They expected everyone else to emulate the citizens in charge of our public affairs."[1]

Isonomia, equality in citizenship, was a central feature of the Athenian conception of democratic government, but as this passage reveals, serious disagreements could and did arise over what this treasured principle should mean in practice. As Phocion had learned earlier in his life, surface appearances were often deceptive, and inquiry into the underlying reality needed to be never-ending. These precepts, he knew, applied strongly in the contention about who ought to decide national policies affecting everyone's shared advantage and benefit.

Phocion experienced a sad personal loss during the Social War when his longtime supporter and friend Chabrias died in a failed Athenian attack against the island of Chios in 357/6. Chabrias had been on a ship that advanced too far ahead of the other Athenian warships when it rushed toward the enemy harbor. When his vessel was rammed so severely that it began to sink, Chabrias refused to jump from the deck into the water and swim to the safety of the friendly vessels behind his. He literally went down with the ship. The military fiasco at Chios generated fierce recriminations in Athens. The overall commander, Chares, accused his colleagues of dereliction of duty for refusing to launch an attack during a storm at sea. The subsequent prosecutions resulted in heavy fines and disgrace for the formerly prominent commanders Iphicrates and Timotheus. As usual, Athenian juries, disheartened by failures in military action, took out their ire on the officers whom they held responsible. The motives and the reality of the alleged culprits' actions were immaterial to their verdict.

The situation in mainland Greece grew much more dangerous through the course of the 350s as the city-states continued their conflicts against one another. At first Athenians hoped that they could again take the lead among the squabbling Greek states because Sparta and Thebes had suffered such devastating losses in the lingering aftermath of the Battle of Mantinea. Soon afterward, the Athenians made an alliance with the Thessalians, whose proximity to Thebes made them hostile to these neighbors in central Greece. In the early 350s, the Athenians regained control of the Chersonese, the narrow peninsula forming the western side of the Hellespont Strait leading to and from the Black Sea. This victory made them much more confident that they could protect the supply of imported grain from that region. At about the same time, they also managed to get the island of Euboea back into their Second League. Euboea's nearby location along the eastern shore of Athenian territory made control of the island crucial for Athens's safety both because it was an important source of grain and also because attacks launched from so close to their territory could come too quickly to allow the Athenians to rally a strong defense.

Meanwhile, a completely unexpected event that had occurred in 359 was to make the situation much more complex. The kingdom of Macedon, which to that point had played a minor role in Greek affairs, suddenly rose to international power. The region called Macedonia would soon give birth to Alexander the Great (356–323), whose career would forever change the character and history of the interactions among southeastern Europe, western and central Asia, and the northeastern corner of Africa. But in the mid-fourth century it was Alexander's father, Philip II (382–336), who first paved the way for the epochal transformation in the international relations of the Greek city-states.

No Greeks at the start of the 350s could have anticipated the storm that was going to descend on them from Macedonia. Situated just north of central Greece, this mountainous land was home to a people who prided themselves on the toughness they had developed to survive the colder climate of their region and to fend off the fierce raids launched against them by their northern and western neighbors. Such wealth as they possessed resided primarily in their access to an abundant supply of timber. The Macedonians regarded themselves as ethnically Greek because they were the descendants of an ancient Hellenic people. Yet they spoke a language that non-Macedonians could not understand, although it was linguistically related to Greek. Macedonians with aspirations to become leaders learned to speak Greek fluently, and inscribed public documents were in Greek.

Almost all their southern Greek neighbors were organized into individual city-states, but the Macedonians lived under the rule of a king. The necessity for Macedonian kings to be wise and tough was rooted in the nature of their rule. Like the Macedonians' general sense of identity, the monarchy based itself on its kings' demonstrating macho charisma. Without it, no king could survive, much less flourish. There was no constitution guaranteeing the succession of a royal family. Instead, to become a king a man had to show that he was tough enough to deserve the loyalty of the leaders of the various baronial clans, social equals who controlled different subregions in Macedonia.

If the king proved manly, fair, and able to organize an effective defense against the Macedonians' violent neighbors, he could rule as their supreme commander — unless one of his rivals launched a successful plot to eliminate him. It was this internal danger that led Macedonian monarchs to station round-the-clock bodyguards at the entrance to their private quarters. If a king survived, he could then pass on his position to a son. That son could rule successfully only if he, too, turned out to be a man's man. He had to prove his worth in the fighting, hunting, and raucous drinking parties that filled male life. Otherwise, a new family might take over the monarchy. Macedonian women from powerful families often took part in the dynastic intrigues and struggles of this system, which bestowed the crown and its benefits only on the strongest families.

The Macedonians' Greek neighbors to the south generally rejected and scorned them. The Athenians remembered the Macedonians as a people whose king had been a vassal of Persia during the Persian Wars and had urged Athens to come to terms with the Great King. The Macedonians' ruler at that time had told the Athenians they could never rally the strength to repel the Persians. It was no surprise, then, that a century and a half later, it became standard rhetorical procedure for Athenian patriots to denounce the ambitions of Macedonian kings. Demosthenes, one of Athens's most vocal speakers urging an aggressive policy to block Philip's plans, once haughtily dismissed him as "not only not a Greek or related to Greeks, but not even a barbarian from a region worth talking about. No, he's a scum from Macedonia, a land where you can't even buy a slave worth his salt." As events were to reveal, no matter how inaccurately and arrogantly the Athenians sneered at Philip's background, it was a terrible misjudgment to underestimate him. Just because Philip was a Macedonian did not mean he was not clever enough or tough enough to dominate them.[2]

Philip proved that he deserved the Macedonian royal title after his brother King Perdiccas and four thousand of his countrymen died in 359 in a battle fighting the army of their northern neighbors. The catastrophic losses incurred by the Macedonian force put their entire land at risk of being pillaged because the dead king had no adult successor ready to take over command. He did have a very young son, however. Philip protected his nephew by defeating other rivals for the throne, one of whom the Athenians had supported, without success. The Macedonian kingdom at this point tottered on the brink of disaster.

At this crucial moment, Philip, though only in his twenties, persuaded the other Macedonian leaders to let him head up a reorganization of the army to save their homeland. He swiftly trained the infantrymen to use a new offensive weapon, a massive thrusting spear called a *sarissa* that was eighteen feet long and weighed about fourteen pounds. Troops had to wield this iron-tipped behemoth with both hands while carrying their shield in front of them strapped on their left arm. They had to learn to make their advances in battle while arranged in the formation of columns and rows of a heavily armed infantry phalanx. They also had to stay precisely spaced so that they did not impale one another with their huge spears. And they had to maintain this alignment in order to move forward together in unison like a giant ram to shatter the enemy's line.

Remarkably, Philip managed in short order to train his men in the strength and discipline needed to attack with this demanding new technology, as well as developing forms of artillery to employ in sieges of enemy settlements and cities. He also taught his infantry to cooperate in the field with cavalry accompanying them to disrupt the opponents' battle order through quick charges on horseback as they hurled javelins and generally harassed the other side's infantry. Philip's tactical innovations succeeded. The Macedonians routed their previously victorious northern enemies and crushed the risk of further threats to the homeland. This unprecedented success guaranteed Philip his status as a respected king. His eventual successor would thereby come from his own line, if that son also proved manfully worthy.

During this period Phocion was most likely elected as a strategos, general, almost every year, so he would have been keenly aware of the rapidly declining odds of Athens's regaining primacy in the strategically important regions to the north. No documentation survives about Phocion's activities when Philip began pursuing his aggressive course to make Macedonia a major player in international politics. The new king successfully extended his power eastward into nearby regions of Thrace, where there were gold mines whose income he appropriated. He also captured the strategically located city-state of Amphipolis, whose appeal to the Athenians for help went unanswered.

When the Second Athenian League lost its strength in the mid-350s, the international situation seemed foreboding to Isocrates, who like Phocion was never shy about criticizing the people for what he regarded as their dangerously self-interested policies. Isocrates proclaimed that the Athenians would prosper only if they stopped trying to build a naval empire and emulated the decidedly less democratic "principles of Sparta's government." The Athenians paid no attention to Isocrates' anti-democracy polemics on how to secure peace in their increasingly unpeaceful world.[3]

Phocion at this stage of his life was well embarked on his long stretch of annual elections as strategos when he took a dramatic, if in the end temporary, turn in his career away from Athens and the generalship. No doubt affected by his grief over Chabrias's death, dismay at the prosecutions of Iphicrates and Timotheus, and above all the stress of being short of money, Phocion in 351/0 accepted a private job as a mercenary commander in a local war on the island of Cyprus in the far eastern Mediterranean. Most remarkable, he fought on the side supporting the Persian Great King. Artaxerxes III had seized the throne in 359/8 after a deadly intrafamily conflict, and during the coming decades he promoted Persia's interests against the growing power of Philip II. A Persian rival eventually murdered Artaxerxes in 338.

Phocion's choice to work for a Persian monarch went against the pronounced and long-standing emphasis in Athenian foreign policy on resisting the power of that imperial ruler, whoever he might be. This is not to say that other Athenians had not worked for a Great King, but Phocion's doing so seems particularly noteworthy. After all, a decade earlier, during the Satraps' Revolt, he had fought alongside Chabrias in opposition to the forces of Artaxerxes II. No matter how disillusioned he had become about the viability of "the people" as the dominant force in Athenian democracy, taking this particular mercenary job on Cyprus seems out of character with his clear dedication to serving his city-state as best he could. Perhaps he judged that Athens had no stake in this particular conflict. In any case, his overriding motivation was surely a pressing need for money. Cyprus was strategically critical to access to eastern Mediterranean regions, an important sector of the Persian Empire. The island was also a major commercial hub, whose heavy seaborne traffic generated a hearty income for whoever controlled it. The Persian king would gladly pay exorbitant wages to protect this vital piece of his empire.

Phocion was most likely the senior commander of the forces fighting the anti-Persian rebels, leading an army that grew to sixteen thousand mercenary soldiers. Many of them joined up because they knew there would be plentiful booty to add to their wages, a financial impetus that presumably appealed to the cash-poor Phocion as well. He served successfully, especially in designing and directing a fortified encampment that laid siege to the major Cypriot city of Salamis. There is no evidence that Phocion ever again worked as a mercenary after this stint. His time on Cyprus apparently proved lucrative enough to solve his financial problems permanently.

Phocion's many terms as strategos also indicate that he reinserted himself into public service upon his return to his homeland following this mercenary episode. Soon he became directly involved in implementing the Athenians' official decision to intervene in a dispute in 348 between two tyrants competing for control of the city of Eretria on the island of Euboea. Philip II supported one of the rivals, which was worrying for the Athenians because if the Macedonian king's favorite should prevail, the threat that Philip represented to them would then extend right up to their eastern border. Nevertheless, Demosthenes opposed Athens's initiative to embroil itself in such a messy conflict. His advice failed to win over the voters. So Phocion was dispatched along with a colleague to head a military force supporting the other competing tyrant, Plutarch by name. He was holding Eretria against his rival Clitarchus.

The Athenian generals found the entire island in an uproar. To make matters worse, they received no military cooperation from Plutarch of Eretria, whom they had been directed to support. Quite a number of Athenian soldiers decided to return home when a major festival began back in Athens. Some others deserted simply because they did not want to fight in this foreign conflict, regardless of its importance for Athens's security. Faced with a manpower leak, Phocion instructed his officers to pay no attention to the shirkers and not to try to stop them from leaving. If these "undisciplined and babbling and good-for-nothing" members of the Athens's citizen militia were forced to stay, he said, they would just get in the way of the valiant and loyal members of the expedition. Furthermore, he added, once they reached Athens they would be too ashamed of their own conduct to lodge official accusations of incompetence about their commanders' or comrades' actions.[4]

The most dramatic battle of the expedition opened with Plutarch prematurely leading his mercenary troops out against the enemy because he had incorrectly assumed that Phocion was delaying an attack due to a lack of courage. In fact, Phocion was purposely proceeding slowly, with mandatory pre-battle sacrifices to the gods, so that his men would remain in the camp. He wanted their opponents to advance imprudently against his fortified position. At precisely the right moment, Phocion ordered his phalanx to advance

beyond the encampment's barricades at top speed. This unanticipated thrust stunned the attackers, many of whom were slain on
the spot. Phocion then commanded some of his men to pause their
attack so that they could provide shelter for Plutarch's troops. Those
soldiers had been put to flight during their commander's premature
advance. The tyrant himself fled the battlefield.

Phocion personally led the best of his troops in a fierce attack
on the enemy's remaining force. A bloody struggle ensued, but his
brigade fought with emotion and without pity, as (the biographer)
Plutarch expressed their valor.[5] They won a decisive victory for their
inspiring commander. He then secured the city of Eretria, banish-
ing the cowardly tyrant Plutarch and taking control of a strategically located fortress to strengthen Athens's defensive perimeter. At
the end of his mission Phocion departed Euboea riding a wave of
success as a perceptive and effective military leader. But unfortunately for the Athenians, the generals whom they sent out to succeed Phocion as commanders on the island failed so miserably that
they were betrayed, kidnapped, and held for an exorbitant ransom
by the very tyrant whom Phocion had expelled.

The debacle on Euboea after Phocion's departure meant that the
Athenians lost control of the island. They therefore now lacked an
important safety net against invasions of their own territory as well
as a crucial source of food. In addition, the financial costs of this
fiasco became so crushing that the daily stipends for jurors on
which the Athenian court system depended had to be suspended.
Feelings in the Assembly remained so bitter over this episode that
Demosthenes subsequently claimed he had been the only person to
speak up against the expedition. He complained that he had been
"for all practical purposes ripped to shreds by the people who wanted
to convince you [the Athenian people] [to launch the military cam-
paign] so that they could haul in small profits."[6]

Yet another grave setback further deteriorated Athens's international position. Since the Athenians depended for their survival on importing supplies from northern regions, they had a long history of striving to protect their national interests by building strong ties with allies there. They even settled members of their own population in communities in this strategically significant area. One especially important northern Greek city-state was Olynthus, located on a prominent peninsula to the east of Macedonia. Athenians had long been involved in the affairs of Olynthus when Philip II began to push aggressively into the Olynthians' territory. They responded by persuading Athens's voters to formalize their two communities' relationship of mutual support.

This development enraged Philip. When he threatened to take Olynthus by force, its residents begged Athens to intervene. Demosthenes and other anti-Philip speakers convinced the Assembly to agree; whether Phocion participated in the debate is not attested. In 348, the Athenians dispatched a considerable force of citizen infantry, mercenaries, and warships to aid Olynthus against Philip. They would have sent more if their public finances had not been so reduced by the expenses of the Euboea expedition. But bad weather slowed the Athenian force's journey of some three hundred miles to reach their ally, and Philip captured Olynthus. In his anger at what he saw as the Olynthians' disloyalty to him, the king destroyed their city. He then dispersed its residents to regions in Macedonia, enslaving many of them to labor on his royal properties. Some of these captives were Athenian hoplites. The dismay in Athens over their men's fate fueled a passion to rouse other Greeks, especially those in the Peloponnese, to unite against the Macedonian menace. But as so often before, the Greeks of the central and southern mainland failed to cooperate with one another.

Sheer desperation now motivated the Athenians to send Philocrates, a politically active contemporary of Phocion, to Macedonia to seek a treaty with Philip. A main goal was to gain the release of their soldiers captured at Olynthus. Philip replied that he would agree to a peace settlement if the Athenians swore to become his allies. Many Athenians were aghast at the prospect of yielding to the demands of such a detested enemy, but this time even Demosthenes spoke in favor of a Phocion-like caution in the interest of safety. His hostility to Philip was second to none, but on this occasion, instead of launching one of his famous *Philippics,* he said that Athens should not go to war with Macedon because its bound-to-lose effort would amount to the mere appearance of valor without any substance. The Assembly, overwhelmed by the risk to Athens, conceded to the Macedonian king's terms. In 346 both sides signed what is called the Peace of Philocrates.

Philip promptly marched into central Greece through the mountain pass at Thermopylae, which the Athenians in 352 had blocked to prevent his progress farther south. Philip then used a display of military power to compel the Thebans and the people of the adjoining region of Phocis to end their violent struggle over control of the sacred oracle of Apollo at Delphi. This tactic ended the so-called Third Sacred War. Philip basked in the glory of acclaim as Apollo's champion and Delphi's savior. He claimed the official leadership of the central Greek region of Thessaly, whose population had recognized him as their archon (ruler) since 352. He also refrained from attacking Thebes. So by the mid-340s, Philip found himself openly opposed only by a weakened Sparta. He was free to scheme to his heart's content if he could find a way to control the notoriously fractious Greeks. That goal proved elusive even for a leader as clever and adaptable as Philip. In Athens, it seems clear that the majority of voters in the Assembly initially stuck to Demosthenes' advice to avoid open confrontation with Philip as agreed to in the Peace of Philocrates. They were, however, ready to do what they could to resist him indirectly.

Phocion's activities as strategos in this period emphasize his commitment to doing all he could as a general to carry out the Assembly's wishes to slow or block Philip's power and influence. In 343, a secret embassy was dispatched from Athens's immediate neighbor to the west, the city-state of Megara. Arriving in the middle of the night, the envoys disclosed to Phocion that two Megarian oligarchs were plotting to put their community into the hands of the Macedonian king. They asked for Athens's help in preventing this. When the Athenian Assembly convened in the morning, Phocion was anxious that the Thebans, now Philip's allies, not hear about the Megarians' appeal to Athens in time to block it militarily. So Phocion, who as we have seen prided himself on making formal speeches in public only when he deemed it absolutely necessary, spoke up in the Assembly and persuaded the voters to agree to aid Megara. Phocion then ordered a trumpeter to blow a call to summon men directly from the Assembly meeting to form up immediately with their arms and armor and march to their neighbor's rescue. The Megarians welcomed the Athenians as soon as they arrived. Phocion organized and oversaw a fast-paced building program of fortifications to protect Megara's port. He ensured that these Long Walls connected the port of Nisaea to Megara's urban center so that the people could import food, continue the maritime mercantile activities on which their economy depended, and guarantee entry to Athenian warships when needed. Phocion's quick decisions and compelling leadership inspired both the Athenians and the Megarians to complete these demanding but essential assignments in record time.

In this same year, 343, Phocion made another demonstration of his ability to act effectively in public when he so chose. This time he served as a character witness in a highly controversial court case. The trial pitted Demosthenes as the prosecutor against Aeschines as the defendant. Demosthenes and Aeschines were by this time prominent politicians, and they detested each other as well as strongly disagreeing about Athens's official posture regarding Philip. Demosthenes was all in for fighting Philip tooth and nail, while Aeschines favored negotiations to achieve some sort of nonviolent coexistence.

The trial had its roots in the Peace of Philocrates. Three years earlier, in 346, Aeschines had been one of the Athenian representatives with Philocrates on the embassy to Philip that led to the king's terms being accepted for the treaty. Since many Athenians believed Philip had exploited the agreement to advance his own interests very aggressively, discontent with the ambassadors had grown over time. In this supercharged political context, another outspoken politician, Hyperides (ca. 390–322), lodged a charge of ambassadorial misconduct against Philocrates. Assessing his chances of acquittal as zero, given the depth of the current political divide in Athens, Philocrates fled the city. His prediction of his fate had been right: he was condemned to death in absentia.

As Athenian legal procedure dictated, prosecutor and defender both had to speak for themselves and, if they could, convince other prominent Athenians to testify on their behalf. Demosthenes, Athens's leading spokesman condemning Philip, had brought his legal charge against Aeschines alleging misconduct during the embassy. In a blistering speech, he impugned Aeschines for betraying Athens's security in return for bribes from Philip. Aeschines in his defense asserted his patriotism and loyalty to his home city-state. To buttress his case, Aeschines recruited several prominent Athenian leaders to speak on his side. One of these was Phocion, whose statement does not survive; it is not recorded whether he expressed his support as a "fellow speaker" (*synegoros*) or in a written document to be read to the jurors. What we do have is Aeschines' description of him: "I call upon Phocion as one of our generals and at the same time as surpassing all of us in his rectitude and justice [dikaiosune]." In other words, Aeschines was counting on the jurors to agree that Phocion was a distinguished commander who could verify Aeschines' own military service on the expedition to Euboea in 348. Aeschines hoped that what Phocion said would be believed because his reputation for integrity in politics was second to none. It is another enigma in the biography of Phocion that by the end of his life a majority of Athenian jurors would conclude the opposite.[7]

Aeschines was correct in thinking that Phocion still enjoyed a level of respect as an incorruptible high public official that made his testimony invaluable. Aeschines was acquitted, though by the narrowest of margins. This infamous trial nevertheless revealed how destructively bitter the Athenians' political disagreements had become now that they were no longer powerful enough to do whatever they wanted in the world. At one point the differing political views of Demosthenes and Phocion produced a startling exchange that laid bare the depth of hostile emotions now in play. Demosthenes chastised his opponent by saying, "The Athenians, Phocion, will kill you if they lose their tempers!" Phocion in response scoffed, "It's you they'll kill, if they have any sense!"[8]

CHAPTER TEN

Enduring a Catastrophe

Phocion's reputation as a staunch defender of Athens's safety continued to grow. Two years after his successful speeches in 343, he led another decisive military action to resist Philip's growing power. A tyrant who aligned himself with Philip had now taken over the city of Eretria on Euboea, where Phocion had previously commanded his Athenian force in 348. This time, in 341, Phocion led his troops to a victory that restored Eretria's democracy. He had devised tactics that minimized the damage inflicted by the enemy's withering artillery fire from catapults atop the city's fortification wall. His military prowess was once again of the highest quality. And his victory came at an age (he was now in his sixties) when Athenian men were no longer expected to go on active service, especially outside the borders of their homeland. His success and his patriotism above and beyond the call of duty without doubt buttressed his reputation. This exploit, too, makes it all the more remarkable that twenty years later he was labeled a traitor.

In 340, Phocion served as a general for Athens on a campaign that directly opposed Philip. This assignment from the Assembly effectively rendered the recent peace agreement a dead letter. The Athenian people had also voted to send Demosthenes as the leader of an embassy to urge the Peloponnesian states to resist Philip, who was trying to seduce oligarchic elites to support him. Philip by now was taking direct action against two of his nominal allies on the approach to the Black Sea, the Greek city-states of Perinthus and Byzantium. He first besieged Perinthus, and when the Byzantines came to Perinthus's aid, he laid siege to Byzantium as well. Both cities appealed to the Athenians for an alliance that would protect them against Macedonian aggression. When the Athenians agreed, Philip attacked a mammoth convoy of 230 cargo ships transporting grain from the Black Sea to Athens through the Hellespont Strait. The Athenians, anxious over their supply chain, openly declared war on Philip.

The Assembly designated Chares as the general to lead a force to help Byzantium. He was a controversial figure, with a reputation for resorting to extreme violence. In 353, for example, Chares had been sent to Sestus on the Hellespont to compel that city to ally with Athens as part of the latter's drive to protect the sea route for its imported grain. Chares not only conquered the city, he massacred the adults and sold the rest of the population into slavery. It is no wonder, then, that suspicion of Chares' motives led the Byzantines to forbid his fleet to enter their harbor. The Athenians became so enraged at this refusal that they were ready to abandon Byzantium to Philip's tender mercies. But then Phocion yet again rose to the speaker's platform. He told his fellow voters they must not be angry at their allies for their lack of trust but rather direct their outrage at the commanders who were distrusted. "They are the ones," he sharply remarked, "who are making you a source of fear to those people who can't be saved except through you!"[1]

Phocion's rebuke changed the voters' minds. He was instructed with two other colleagues to lead an expedition to aid Athens's allies in the Hellespont region in 340/39. At Byzantium, Phocion met up with Leon, an old friend from that city who had been a fellow student with him at Plato's Academy. Leon had so much confidence in Phocion's trustworthiness that he persuaded his compatriots to allow his friends' troops to enter their fortified city instead of having to build a camp outside its walls. Safely ensconced inside Byzantium, Phocion and his Athenian colleagues launched successful attacks against the forces of Philip. The Macedonian king only barely managed to extricate his army from a catastrophic defeat by confusing his Greek opponents about the route he intended to take in retreat. Phocion then began a series of successful raids on Macedonian-held territory in this northern coastal region. He eventually had to withdraw because he himself received a wound serious enough to require him to rest. He sailed home in 338. As had occurred after the Battle of Naxos years earlier, at Byzantium Phocion had been accepted as a friendly and reliable Athenian by Greeks who had reason to suspect the motives and intent of leaders from his city-state. It seems a continuing motif of Phocion's life that he often got along better with Greeks from other communities than he did with a significant percentage of the people at home.

It is a coincidence worthy of ancient Greek epic poetry that 338, the year of Phocion's return to Athens after his campaign-ending battle injury, also turned out to be a history-changing time for all Greeks east of Italy. This was the effect of the infamous Battle of Chaeronea in Boeotia, the region just north of Athens. The immediate cause of this salient event came from Philip's exploitation for his own purposes of another intra-Greek dispute. On the pretense of acting to protect the Oracle of Apollo at Delphi, he led an army southward into central Greece. The news of his arrival there had created such dire panic in Athens that a giant crowd rushed to the

Assembly. The citizens' fright was so great that no one dared step onto the speaker's platform to advise them on the best course of action—until Demosthenes took the podium. He rejected negotiations with Philip, and the Assembly sent him to Thebes to plead for help in finding a way to stop the Macedonian king.[2] Astonishingly, the Thebans agreed to join their frequent enemies in preparing for war against this formidable opponent.

That was the situation when Phocion arrived home from the mission in the north during which he had been injured. When Demosthenes urged the Assembly to go to war swiftly so that the fight against Philip could take place as far from Athenian territory as possible, Phocion chided him. "Oh sir," he responded, "let's not think about where we can go to battle, but how we can win. That's how war can stay far away from us—for if we lose, each and every horror will be right on top of us!" Phocion counseled postponing open conflict by responding to Philip's new offer to discuss terms. No one could have accused the war hero Phocion of cowardice or ignorance when he made this recommendation. After all, he had a recent wound as proof of his courage and his knowledge of this enemy. But Demosthenes' position prevailed.[3]

The Athenians therefore decided to send troops to Chaeronea to oppose Philip, joining the Thebans and some smaller contingents from other Greek states. Phocion was not made one of the generals commanding Athens's troops, perhaps because his political rivals wanted to deprive him of the opportunity to add to his military reputation. As it turned out, the Greek alliance could have profited from his demonstrated excellence as a commander in battle.

The value of Phocion's insight that it was not the time to take the field against the Macedonians became clear when Philip outgeneraled the Greek allies at Chaeronea in the early fall of 338. Philip's eighteen-year-old son Alexander played a key role in the Macedonian victory by leading a successful charge that broke the ranks of Thebes's elite corps of warriors, the Sacred Band. This group was famed for being composed of 150 pairs of male lovers. By the end of the day, the Macedonian rout of the combined Greek forces was complete. So awful were its consequences felt to be over time at Athens that the orator Lycurgus (ca. 390–324) later lamented this decisive defeat and the deaths of so many at Chaeronea by remarking that "at the very moment that they died, the condition of Greece descended into slavery!"[4]

When the distressing news of the calamity reached Athens, a fierce division erupted over what to do. Demosthenes, who at this time wielded the most influence with the Assembly despite his complaint that the always concise Phocion was "the pruning knife of my speeches," uncharacteristically kept out of this crucial debate. Demosthenes was perhaps cowed because his political rivals had spread a rumor that he had dropped his armor in fright and fled for home when the tide of battle at Chaeronea turned against the Greeks. Nevertheless, the many men who respected Demosthenes persuaded the Assembly to appoint him to deliver the public funeral oration that Athens regularly held to honor its war dead.[5]

The tension in Athens immediately after Chaeronea rose sky high. When Lycurgus blamed the general Lysicles for the defeat and rebuked him for daring to remain alive as a reminder of their homeland's shame and disgrace, the people voted to execute Lysicles. Hyperides proposed radical measures to beef up Athens's defense: give citizenship to all foreigners in the city and liberate the slaves to motivate both groups for military service, and confine women and children within the fortifications of Piraeus for their protection. Next some citizens grabbed Charidemus, a mercenary commander from Euboea who had been made an Athenian citizen as a reward for previous service supporting the city-state. They pushed him to the front of the Assembly, shouting that he should be made a general to lead a counterattack against Philip. This proposal put terror into the hearts of the elite citizens. They rallied the members of the Council of the Areopagus to join them in tearfully begging the voters to protect their community by taking a radically different approach: they should "entrust the polis to Phocion!"[6]

In practice, this dramatic proposal meant agreeing to listen carefully to Phocion's advice. It did not mean overturning the democratic governmental structure of Athens. Unlike the contemporary Romans, the Athenians had no provision for emergency martial law. They lacked any office comparable to the Romans' time-delimited *dictator*, which bestowed temporary total power on a single leader to organize a swift response to an imminent military threat. In the crisis created by Philip's victory at Chaeronea, Phocion was acknowledged to be Athens's best guide about what to do in a desperate situation. He knew from reading the historian Thucydides that the famous statesman Pericles a century earlier had told the Athenians to accept danger to fight for their independence even when war and plague had joined together to weaken them. But he now felt compelled to recommend a melancholy realism instead. To preserve Athens from total destruction, he told the voters, they must agree to whatever terms Philip imposed rather than try to muster another armed response.

In return, Philip offered Athens a deal. While celebrating his triumph at Chaeronea, the Macedonian monarch had become wildly inebriated and stumbled over to where Greek captive soldiers were being detained so he could make fun of them as pitiful losers. One of these prisoners was Demades (ca. 380–ca. 318), an Athenian known for his sharp tongue in addressing the Assembly. Unbowed by the Macedonian king's slurred insults, Demades loudly rebuked Philip by referring to Homer's story of the Trojan War: "O king, when Luck has given you the role of Agamemnon, aren't you ashamed to behave like Thersites?" Since Agamemnon was the Greek's supreme military commander at the siege of Troy while Thersites was a soldier from the ranks whom his colleagues mocked for his lack of discipline, Demades was casting shame on Philip's behavior as unworthy of a truly noble leader. Astonishingly, Philip upon hearing these words citing Homer's revered epic ceased his drunken showing off and declared Demades free to return home. The king notified the Athenians that he would free all his Athenian prisoners without ransom, that he would not invade Attica, and that he would make a formal peace with them if they disbanded the Second Athenian League and joined his alliance. Phocion approved this plan, and his fellow voters complied.[7]

Phocion's motivation throughout this risky time for Athens seems, as always, to have been to preserve his city-state rather than profit from his prominence. At some point after the Battle of Chaeronea (the exact date is not recorded), Philip sent a very large sum of money to Phocion, an obvious attempt to buy his continuing support. Phocion, however, turned it down despite the entreaties of Philip's representatives that he take the cash for the benefit of his children. Phocion told them, "If my offspring are going to be different from me, then I don't want their luxury to be fed and increased at my expense." Phocion clearly treasured his devotion to what he saw as his personal integrity above a luxurious lifestyle. As future events would reveal, his choice to turn down bribes was not a universal one for Athenian leaders claiming to support their city-state's democracy against foreign foes.[8]

Thebes and Sparta fared far less well than Athens following the Battle of Chaeronea. Philip had the Theban leaders who opposed him executed and installed a Macedonian garrison on the city's citadel to keep its citizens under tight rein. He also threatened to invade the Peloponnese and ravage the territory of Sparta. He refrained from ousting Sparta's government only because, so the story went, he received a sign from the healing god Asclepius to desist. Finally, Philip announced to the Greeks that he was organizing a new Greek League with himself as its (allegedly) voluntarily chosen leader (*hegemon*). He scheduled a conference to be held at Corinth in 336 to confirm his plans for the alliance and a shared peace. This arrangement mimicked the form of traditional Greek leagues whose members joined voluntarily, but in truth it was a veil for Philip's military dominance over the city-states. It was also meant to be the vehicle for his soon to be proclaimed expedition against the Persian Empire. The pretext for this mission was to exact vengeance for the Persian Wars, but actually he was aiming for glory and wealth. Demades urged the Athenians to accept Philip's terms. Phocion by contrast advised the Assembly to hold off agreement until Philip made clear what he was going to require his allies to contribute in terms of manpower and resources to support his ambitions for immortal fame. The Athenians this time decided to listen to Demades and agreed to sign on as members of Philip's new panhellenic League of Corinth.

This consequence of their defeat at Chaeronea deeply distressed most Athenians. They chafed at the damage done to their formerly leading place in their world by the Macedonian kingdom's ascent to prominence and power in international relations. Even though allying with Philip allowed them to retain their traditional form of democratic government, they hated the infringement on their autonomy of action in foreign policy imposed by membership in Philip's new league. But they reluctantly accepted that they had no real choice under the circumstances. At the Corinth meeting, Philip proclaimed his ambitious plan for invading Persia and ordered his new allies to supply troops and ships for the mammoth effort. The Athenians' jaws collectively dropped when they heard how much they would have to spend to provide the cavalry and triremes that Philip demanded. When they began discussing rebellion against this burden, Phocion intervened. "This is just what I was afraid of when I spoke against your joining Philip's league," he told them. "Now that you have agreed to do that, however, you can't back down or lose heart. Remember that our ancestors were sometimes the ones in charge, sometimes the ones under orders, and by filling both these roles with distinction they secured safety for our city-state and the Greeks."[9]

If it had not been clear earlier that Phocion was foundationally a realist in his patriotism, it certainly was now. Resistance against daunting odds amounted to national suicide, he believed. No matter the amount of disdain or disgust that he as a member of the Athenian social elite might have felt about what he regarded as the usually foolish and corrupted predispositions of the people, his actions document that he had no wish to see them destroyed. If only they had felt the same about him, his ultimate fate might well have been different.

Some modern scholars label the outcome of the Battle of Chaeronea as signaling the end of the freedom of the Greek city-states of the fifth and fourth centuries BCE. This assessment would make the event the closing moment of the history of Classical Greece (a term derived from the value-judgment labels assigned to notional periods in the history of ancient Greek art and architecture). In fact, it is an overstatement. Most Greek city-states continued to operate largely as they had in the past in terms of determining their internal governance and domestic policies. It was now true, however, that their foreign policy was no longer solely under their own control.

The question of what the new requirement that Greek city-states cooperate with the Macedonian king on international policy was going to mean in practice took on new urgency during the unprecedented events of the career of Alexander, Philip's son. That career began in a climate of murder and suspicion. In 336, after dispatching an advance force to western Asia Minor to open the way for a full-scale attack on Persian territory, Philip acted to promote regional stability for Macedonia during his anticipated prolonged absence on campaign abroad. He arranged a lavish public ceremony to celebrate a diplomatic marriage between one of his daughters and the king of Epirus, west of Macedonia. To display his confidence in his supreme status as leader of a large alliance of Greeks, Philip entered the ceremony ostentatiously in advance of his usual bodyguards. One of those protectors of the king was a young man who blamed Philip for his public humiliation when he was raped by one of the king's top lieutenants. This armed youth leaped ahead and stabbed Philip to death in revenge. The assassin died at the hands of guards who rushed up too late to save their king.

Competition among the Macedonian elite for the kingship was of course the rule, and assassination was far from unknown as a tactic. Some people whispered that Alexander had been in on the plot to kill his father so he could succeed to the throne. Alexander did manage to maneuver his older half-brother Philip Arrhidaeus (359–317) out of the running to become the new king, probably because his sibling was known to have learning disabilities that rendered him incapable of handling the constant challenges confronting a Macedonian ruler. Alexander kept Arrhidaeus alive, however. Others whom Alexander judged to be potential threats to his ascension did not survive the transition.

Local unrest over this unexpected political turmoil in Macedonia was far from the only problem that the twenty-year-old Alexander faced in trying to take over his father's kingdom and his plans for conquest using the League of Corinth. The Greeks to the south rejoiced at what they saw as their liberation from a tyrant's grip. Demosthenes, who heard about Philip's murder before the news reached Athens publicly, told the Council of Five Hundred that he had had a dream promising good luck for Athens. When messengers then arrived with the full story of the assassination, Demosthenes put a garland on his head and proposed an official declaration honoring Philip's killer. Phocion, who was then doing a year's public service as a member of the council, spoke out to denounce Demosthenes' behavior at this event. He chided his fellow citizens as uncouth for celebrating a murder with joy. After all, he concluded, the power marshaled against them at Chaeronea had now been reduced by only one person.

Phocion's anxiety proved well founded. Defying expectations that a man as young as he could effectively lead an army against seasoned opponents, Alexander quickly outflanked the forces that were trying to block his progress into central Greece. The Greeks now had to acknowledge him as the League of Corinth's hegemon. The Athenians prevented damage to Attica by suing Alexander for peace. Alexander granted their request without imposing any penalties. He then summoned the representatives of the Greek city-states to Corinth to renew their commitment to the league and to designate him their leader in its revenge invasion of Persia's empire.

With the Greeks now formally pacified, Alexander turned north of Macedonia to repel the attempts by enemies in Thrace and Illyria to ravage the territory of a the new young king. In a series of daring campaigns, Alexander eliminated these threats. First, he marched as far north as the Danube River. He shocked his opponents into retreat by crossing over this major geographical boundary and ravaging their nearby settlement. To mark the spot where he decreed his enemies should never again cross to attack Macedonia, he sacrificed to Zeus the Savior, to his famed son Heracles, and to the river god of the Danube. Soon thereafter, Alexander turned westward. In 335, in the non-Greek territory northwest of central Greece, a coalition of fierce tribes put on a massive campaign that seemed likely to overwhelm his force. Fooling them with a faked retreat, he all but obliterated them with a surprise counterattack at night.

In a world without rapid communication of international news, the Greeks to the south heard nothing accurate about Alexander's successes. Demosthenes even produced a fake witness who claimed Alexander had been killed in a northern battle. The Thebans, hating the garrison on their urban citadel that Philip had imposed on them, decided to rebel against the league in 335. Encouraged by some Athenian leaders, including Demosthenes, the Thebans murdered two top officers of the Macedonian force who had walked down into the main city. The Thebans followed up this act of defiance by blockading the remaining foreign troops garrisoning the citadel. Their rebellion encouraged other Greeks to follow the Thebans' example. The Athenians opted to ship weapons to Thebes to strengthen the rebels.

These Greeks had disastrously underestimated their league's new leader. Alexander marched his troops three hundred miles from Illyria to Thebes in less than two weeks. In Athens, Demosthenes began condemning Alexander as a deadly threat that had to be stopped. Phocion strongly disagreed, beginning his objection by quoting Homer's *Odyssey* to his political rival: "Oh, you horrible person, why do you want to enrage a savage man?" and then adding in his own words, "The world is on fire right in front of us, and you want to fan the flames? I keep on doing my job as a general specifically to prevent these people [the Athenians] from being killed even if they are willing!" This comment again points to an unmistakable characteristic of Phocion as a leader and political adviser at Athens. He made decisions that flatly contradicted the people's wishes whenever he concluded that he knew better than they what was in their best interest to keep them safe.[10]

Upon reaching Thebes, Alexander encamped in front of the city without attacking immediately. Instead, he announced to the population that he wanted them to cooperate with him and the other Greeks. When they responded by having a herald from atop their city wall denounce Alexander as "the tyrant of Greece," this insult infuriated the young king. A fierce battle ensued in which Alexander's army killed six thousand Thebans. Alexander then assembled representatives of the Greek states of the league to certify Thebes's fate: enslavement of the survivors and total destruction of the city. In the wake of this horror, the king also sent word to the Athenians demanding the surrender of ten of their leaders who had criticized and opposed him. The list included Demosthenes and Charidemus.[11]

Phocion now became a major figure in the tense situation between Alexander and Athens. When the Assembly sought his advice on how to respond to Alexander's demand, Phocion made a remarkable reply. Blaming his political rivals for having caused the crisis, he said he would surrender even his own best friend if that were required, adding, "And if I myself could die on behalf of all of you, I would see that as good luck. . . . It is better for us and for those who escaped from Thebes to persuade and to implore those who hold dominance than it is to fight." He bluntly demanded that the men surrender themselves to Alexander to save the city of their birth. He accused them of "unmanliness and cowardice" for not immediately doing so.[12]

These were truly fightin' words in Athenian discourse. Legal charges could be brought against a person who accused another of being a coward. The Athenians prided themselves on their tradition of saying whatever they wanted (*parrhesia,* usually translated as "freedom of speech"), but they were also acutely aware of the power of words to do harm by arousing passionate emotions that could lead to disgrace and violence. Like everyone in Athens, Phocion would have known that the modern nursery rhyme "Sticks and stones may break my bones, but words can never hurt me" is and has always been an utterly empty claim. Tumult accordingly ensued in the Assembly meeting, and Phocion was booed off the speaker's platform. Eventually, the voters were persuaded to send a mission to Alexander to beg him to spare the men whom he had demanded be sent to him. Probably both Phocion and Demades were dispatched to make this plea. Phocion seems to have persuaded Alexander to save Athens's citizens. He convinced Alexander that the best way to acquire the fame the new king so fervently desired was to pay no further attention to the mainland Greeks in order to focus on attacking Persia.

Alexander apparently was so impressed by Phocion that he formally recognized him as a friend (*philos*), the term that Macedonian kings used for people especially valued by them. He also designated Phocion as a guest or host (*xenos*), the Greek term for a special contact in a foreign community. After Alexander left for Asia, he wrote Phocion letters, which always bore a uniquely warm expression of greeting. Alexander even sent Phocion a personal gift of one hundred talents, a life-altering sum. This immense total equaled some two thousand years' wages for a decently paid worker. When Phocion asked Alexander's representatives why he was chosen from among all the Athenians to receive such a treasure, they replied that the king thought he was the only fine and good man in the city.

A "fine and good man" in Athenian parlance designated a member of the social elite who behaved honorably according to ancestral tradition as opposed to following the debased norms of the many. The appellation reeked of class prejudice. It is therefore revealing that Phocion in declining this king's ransom replied to Alexander's envoys, "Well then, may he allow me both always to seem that type of person and to be that type of person." When they persisted, he added, "If I make use of this money, I will discredit the king and myself." Alexander was unhappy when he heard Phocion had rejected the cash — making big gifts to others was a traditional way for ancient kings to display their superiority to the recipients. He nevertheless did eventually agree to Phocion's request that, instead of sending him money, Alexander would release several prominent Greeks imprisoned on diverse charges. Evidently Phocion believed that Athens could petition Alexander for favors, but he rejected any initiatives to oppose the ruler openly.[13]

Alexander left the Greek mainland for his campaign against the Persian Empire in 334, marching inexorably farther and farther east for nearly the next ten years. He defeated the Great King in the latter's homeland and then pushed on eastward instead of turning back for home. Alexander aimed to keep going until he discovered the ends of the earth, but his troops, disabled by sheer exhaustion and homesickness, finally refused to go a step farther than northwestern India. Frustrated nearly out of his mind, Alexander marched them south to the Indian Ocean for sacrifices to the gods. He then conducted a large contingent on an exhausting march back on foot through a fierce desert to present-day Iraq. Arriving in 324, he began planning a new search to explore the (to him) still unknown regions of the world, in an expedition directed toward the lands to the far west.

CHAPTER ELEVEN

Approaching the Beginning of the End

Relative calm prevailed in Greece in the decade following Alexander's departure for Asia in 334. The mainland Greek city-states used this largely peaceful period to rebuild much of the prosperity they had lost in the years of war preceding the launch of the Macedonian king's expedition. Sparta openly tried to defy Alexander's arrangements for Greece by starting a small-scale revolt in 331, which Athens did not join. Antipater (400–319), the Macedonian commander whom Alexander had assigned to oversee Macedonia and Greece, crushed the rebels. Their defeat was so decisive that no other Greeks during Alexander's lifetime made any attempt to escape his regime's dominance. When Alexander, far away in Asia, was informed about the Spartans' rebellion, he dismissed it derisively: "It seems while we have been defeating Darius [the king of Persia] here, there has been a battle of mice back home."[1]

The Athenians made no such miscalculations about their chances of evading their detested obligation to profess loyalty to Alexander. There is relatively little evidence for the Athenians' political activity during the final ten years of Alexander's life in the late 330s and 320s, when Lycurgus held the preeminent position in Athenian politics. Lycurgus was certainly strongly supportive of Athens's democracy, but as a political leader he seems to have avoided provoking Antipater.

Through Lycurgus's influence the Athenians created a new system of regulating public finance as a support for political stability. They created an office for this duty; the controller of finances served a four-year term rather than the traditional single year. The voters had concluded that the stress of the times after Chaeronea called for such an innovation in governmental structure. Lycurgus, a noted orator who did not always see eye to eye with Phocion even though they had both been students in Plato's Academy, held this new office three times in a row. He was a success. Inscriptions and archaeology document a robust building program that he spearheaded during this period. Construction projects included major structures for holding games and exhibitions in honor of Athena, a large storehouse for naval equipment at Piraeus, and a renovation of the Theater of Dionysus, where plays, musical performances, and other central events of Athenian public life took place. Additionally, the navy was expanded to a reported four hundred triremes. This expensive project indicates that a great deal of money was now available for warship construction and equipment as well as wages for crews. In addition, a formal public program was created for training ephebes, the eighteen- to twenty-year-old men preparing for military service.

A man confident in the rightness of his opinions, Lycurgus also sponsored morality legislation. Among other laws was one that forbade women to be carried in chariots at the celebration of the Mysteries of Demeter; when his own wife ignored this restriction, he had her fined. A number of prominent Athenians found Lycurgus overbearing, and he was often involved in legal suits. Alexander also suspected Lycurgus of continuing to promote the same anti-

Macedonian views that the Athenians had manifested while Philip was alive. His suspicion had led Alexander to include Lycurgus among the group of Athenians whom the new king had wanted to punish in 335. Lycurgus had orally attacked Phocion in the Assembly on that occasion for his view that the ten men should surrender themselves to save Athens. Once Alexander had crossed over to Asia, however, Lycurgus was out of danger and continued his oversight of the strengthening of Athens's financial resources.

Lycurgan Athens, as modern scholars call it, represented a relatively quiet and prosperous time for Athenians compared with earlier periods of Phocion's life. Phocion was now approaching seventy, but must have continued holding the office of strategos even during these later years. Given the relative calm in Greece during this period, there was no call for him as a general to lead troops into combat. The Athenians certainly had to keep on Alexander's good side, which in practice meant not provoking scrutiny from his agent Antipater. As Alexander's deputy, Antipater controlled a strong force to compel obedience when necessary. A main requirement for Athens to remain in Alexander's favor was that the city-state abide by the terms imposed on the Greek allies in the League of Corinth. On one occasion Alexander wrote a letter to the Athenians instructing them to send him triremes, and some Athenian politicians opposed the order because of the large cost and because, moreover, few Athenians wanted to sail to the Asian coasts to fight a sea battle in support of the young king's ambitions. When the Council of Five Hundred asked Phocion for his advice, he expressed what had become his uniformly realistic policy: "Well, I say to you either dominate with your weapons, or be friends with those who dominate." Athens ended up sending a large number of warships to serve under Alexander's command, whose crews therefore became subject to the Macedonian's judgment.[2]

Phocion's advice on the ships, offered in his characteristically sharp-edged style of expression, represented what he saw as the only possible course for securing Athens's safety: avoid conflict with those stronger than we are. Athenians who disagreed probably denigrated him as a defeatist for advocating subservience to a foreign master. These disagreements could achieve a potent level of verbal venom (anticipating the rhetorical evocations of bloody violence currently commonplace in U.S. politics). One example of the poisonous Athenian in-fighting came in a clash of words between Phocion and Pytheas, a much younger Athenian with aspirations for political prominence, known for opposing Demosthenes' anti-Macedonian policies. The famously concise Phocion, exasperated at what he apparently regarded as Pytheas's long-winded addresses, exclaimed, "Won't you shut up about this, you newly purchased slave to the demos!" The odd aspect of this story is that Pytheas was thought to be virulently pro-Macedonian in his views, which means that presumably he would have agreed with Phocion that Athens should not take any action that could be seen as rebellion against Alexander's regime. Most likely Phocion had become irritated by Pytheas because he suspected him of siding with Alexander not based on any sense of a patriotic realism but rather from a desire for personal profit through gifts from the king.[3]

In sum, the return of Lycurgan Athens to relative prosperity did little to stem the tremendous psychological impact of the loss of Athens's once unchallenged superiority in power, wealth, and pride among the city-states of mainland Greece. Athenians longingly remembered those days of glory. They had always believed that their feeling of belonging, of their autochthonous Athenian identity, marked them out as special. But now that memory seemed increasingly distant. Eloquent evidence for this feeling comes from a court speech that Aeschines made in 330 when he became embroiled in another intense legal fight with Demosthenes. The issue between them boiled down in personal terms to a feud over whose honor was greater, but at the same time a major difference regarding public policy also separated them. Aeschines provided a lengthy, dolorous description of what he saw as the rock-bottom level to which Athens had sunk as Macedonian power had risen. He explicitly blamed this decline on Demosthenes' advice and actions. In the following excerpt, Aeschines describes what he saw as the prevailing mood in Athens in the early and mid-320s while Alexander was attacking the Persian Empire even while the city-state's material condition improved:

> And so what unthinkable or unanticipated event has failed to occur in our time? We haven't had normal human lives but were given life to be a source of stories of marvels for generations in the future. Isn't it so that the Persian king, the one who dug a channel through Mount Athos [to aid his navy in the Persian Wars], who put a yoke on the Hellespont, who demanded earth and water from the Greeks [as a sign of submission], who had the audacity in his letters to write that he was the master of all peoples from the rising to the setting sun, is toiling not to become the ruler of other people but now to save his own life? . . . And Thebes, Thebes, the city that is a neighbor to us, has been torn away from the center of Greece in just one day. That was just, it may well be, because they pursued a totally wrong policy, but their blindness and madness didn't come from a human source — it was from the gods. . . . And our city, the shared refuge of the Greeks, which in times past received ambassadors from the rest of Greece, each embassy seeking to secure protection from us for their individual cities, is no longer a competitor for the leading position among the Greeks but is now struggling just to keep its own land.[4]

Even though Aeschines overwhelmingly lost the vote in his case against Demosthenes, it is important to recognize that the emotions he expressed about Athens's loss of independence and pride remained widespread and passionate among his fellow citizens. Aeschines' plaintive description of the fate of Athens echoed through the speeches and writings of Phocion's contemporaries for the years during which the reports of Alexander's victories and explorations in the East continued to astonish his world. Recognizing this state of affairs helps us anticipate why Phocion experienced such powerful blowback to his recommendations regarding Athenian policy after the death of Alexander in 323.

Before that, however, in 324 a sign of hope appeared that Alexander, the conquering juggernaut, might somehow falter. In that year, Harpalus, a Macedonian who had served as Alexander's treasurer managing the unimaginable amounts of booty the king accumulated on his expedition, fled from Asia to Greece. Harpalus had been spending the king's money on a fantastically expensive and dissolute life for himself far behind the front lines when he was supposed to be safeguarding the conqueror's mountains of money and valuables. Fearing punishment from Alexander once the king returned to Persia from India, Harpalus took off for Greece, bringing with him the vast sum of six thousand talents, numerous mercenary soldiers, and a fleet of triremes. He tried to convince the Athenians to let him enter their port, but they refused, fearing the size of his military forces. They also knew Alexander would be furious if they gave sanctuary to this mega-thief. Harpalus sailed away to the Peloponnese, where he paid off his entourage so that he could return to Athens with a single ship carrying seven hundred talents.

This time the Athenians admitted Harpalus, even though Alexander had sent agents to capture the runaway. The reason the majority of citizens might have changed their minds about taking in

Harpalus was their outrage at Alexander's concurrent proclamation, called the Exiles Decree. It required Greek city-states to take back citizens whom they had previously exiled for disloyalty; Alexander's goal was presumably to reduce the chances that these displaced people would be driven by the insecurity of their circumstances to conduct raids and revolts, thus destabilizing the region. Many of these exiles had become mercenaries in the Macedonian army, but now, with Alexander's Asian campaign winding down, they needed somewhere to live. The Athenians were horrified at the prospect of having to reintegrate these men into their democracy. Furthermore, since many of the exiles had had their property confiscated when they were expelled, they would now demand restitution. And the Athenians also faced a special problem: forty years earlier they had settled their own people on the Aegean island of Samos. By the terms of Alexander's decree, those Athenians would now have to abandon their Samian properties and return home. Turmoil seemed guaranteed if the policy mandated by Alexander went into effect.

The Athenians' anxiety about their relations with Alexander became still more acute in 324 when they received the message that the Macedonian conqueror wanted the Greek city-states to recognize him as a god. The issue of how to categorize Alexander's deification was complex and controversial then and remains so now in modern scholarship. One very short take on this issue is that Greeks saw humans and gods not as totally distinct in their natures but rather as existing at the opposite ends of a spectrum of being. As the early poet Hesiod (fl. between 850 and 750) had taught, deities and mortal beings derive from the same source. The famous divinity Dionysus, for example, had been born human and then reborn as a god, while the semi-divine Heracles, a son of Zeus, had been fully divinized after his death to join the gods on Olympus.

Alexander was asking to be recognized not just locally but

throughout much of the Greek world as a present incarnation of that spectrum, to be a god while also remaining a human being who kept company with human beings. He had earned this status, in his mind, by having out-achieved all previous human beings with his exploits. At Athens, Demosthenes reportedly told the Assembly, "Let Alexander be the son of Zeus, and of Poseidon, too, if that is what he wants." This sort of sarcasm would have been dangerous if it were communicated to Alexander, so the Athenians' official position was acceptance of Alexander's request. What Phocion thought of the situation is recorded in no ancient source. Most likely he agreed that Athens's safety required acquiescence.[5]

Harpalus's presence exacerbated the increasingly fraught circumstances in which the Athenians found themselves that year. To try to secure his own personal safety, Harpalus resolved to hand out the money that he had brought with him from Asia to any influential leader ready to take a payment under the table. He started by trying to win over Phocion, telling the Athenian that he could have sole control of the seven hundred talents stolen from Alexander. The implication was that Phocion could use this vast sum to benefit himself as well as the city-states. Phocion pointedly warned Harpalus of the consequences of such actions, which could destroy the city-state. In referring to the damage that bribery of political leaders could do to Athens's democracy, Phocion turned out to be presciently on the mark.

Demosthenes and other leading Athenians persuaded the Assembly to confiscate the entire sum and secure it in a storeroom on the Acropolis. When the Council of the Areopagus subsequently conducted an accounting in response to allegations of peculation by leading Athenians (including Demosthenes), the shocking news emerged that there were now only 350 talents in storage. Lawsuits and accusations of corruption began flying in every direction. One target was Phocion's son-in-law. When he came to trial, he asked Phocion to defend him. Phocion refused, saying he had admitted the younger man into his family only for doing what was right; he evidently refused to help his son-in-law as a result of his own dedication to respecting justice. Phocion himself came under suspicion: even in the absence of any evidence that he might have accepted a bribe, some of his fellow citizens continued to suspect him of also having been seduced by the lure of illicit cash.

Unfounded in Phocion's case, this suspicion turned out to be true in the case of Demosthenes. He was disgraced when it emerged that in his role as official guardian of the treasure he had appropriated twenty talents (an enormous sum) for himself. Hyperides and others prosecuted the renowned orator and self-declared patriot for corruption. They won their case, and Demosthenes was fined fifty talents. Unable to pay the fine, he was put into confinement but managed to escape and fled Athens. Harpalus got away too, but not long afterward he was murdered by one of his comrades. Enduring damage had been done to Athens. Divisions and disagreements among its citizens now roiled with even fiercer energy.

And then in 323, a completely unexpected bombshell exploded that did the seemingly impossible by making the politically volatile situation at Athens even more uncertain: news arrived that Alexander had died in Babylon a month before his thirty-third birthday. Most likely he fell victim to disease, but stories reflecting the traditional deadly conflicts of the Macedonian royal court insisted that he had been poisoned to make way for a rival. The notoriously pro-Macedonian Demades derided the report as false, remarking that if the king really were dead, the entire world would long before have been permeated by the smell emanating from his corpse. Many Athenians, however, were delighted to believe that Alexander was gone. Speaker after speaker rushed to the podium in the Assembly to urge rebellion against Macedonian control, a move that would mean war with Antipater. Phocion spoke out against any rash decision: "Well, if Alexander is dead today, he will also be dead tomorrow and then the day after that, so we can make plans at our leisure, and with more safety." Phocion was, as always, advocating that his fellow citizens pursue whatever course of action – or inaction – was most likely to preserve Athens from disaster. Whether in the long run he was always right to reject war as an option until it was clear there was no other choice is a question that seems especially relevant in the context of events to come.[6]

Once Alexander's premature death was confirmed, the majority of Athenians decided to initiate a rebellion against the League of Corinth and its Macedonian oversight of them. Other Greek states followed their lead. They hoped to take advantage of what they thought would be confusion among the Macedonians over who was now their monarch. Alexander's wife, Roxane, was pregnant, but her son (as the child turned out to be) had not yet been born; he would be known as Alexander IV following his birth in late 323 or early 322. In the meantime, Alexander's brother Philip Arrhidaeus became the active king, known as King Philip III of Macedon. But Philip's permanent mental disabilities kept him from assuming a leadership role.

In this atmosphere of uncertainty, Athens hired several thousand mercenaries from Alexander's Asia expedition who had been gathered earlier by Leosthenes of Athens, who had a history of opposition to Macedonian rule over Greeks. Antipater in Macedonia was the immediate threat to their newly declared independence. Phocion openly opposed the preparations for war against Antipater, who had now begun to advance south with his troops to subdue the rebel Greek states. Feelings in Athens ran high, with some members of the social elite counseling restraint but the majority of the people rallying in the Assembly for a return to the glory days when the Athenians had led the drive against "barbarian" threats to win freedom for all Greeks. They were intent on fighting a Hellenic war.

Phocion bluntly expressed his rejection of military action against Antipater. The fervidly anti-Macedonian orator Hyperides then confronted Phocion publicly, asking, "Well then, Phocion when *are* you going to advise us Athenians to go to war?" Phocion caustically replied, "Whenever I see our young men willing to maintain their positions in the battle line, our rich inhabitants contributing for war expenses, and our orators refraining from stealing public funds!" As Phocion went on to explain, he foresaw that Athens lacked the resources to prevail in a war of any length. Disastrously for his homeland, Phocion's prediction came true, though not for some time.[7]

At first the military situation in 323–322 swung in Athens's favor. The Greeks to the north obstructed Antipater's campaign southward, and the reinforcements he had summoned from Macedonian forces in Asia were slow to reach him. The Athenians at this point kept Phocion in Attica rather than sending him north for reasons that remain unclear; perhaps some feared he might accept a deal on Antipater's terms. When an enemy force began to ravage the Attic coastline, however, Phocion was given the command. Just as he had predicted, the Athenian soldiers in the city's force showed themselves undisciplined and loath to follow orders in battle. Somehow, however, he induced enough of his men to cooperate, and under his command, they put the Macedonians and their mercenaries to flight and killed their commander. Phocion's military success was a notable achievement in leadership for an eighty-year-old general.

Prospects for Athens seemed to soar when the army of Greek allies defeated Antipater's forces in battle near the central Greek city of Lamia (hence the modern name Lamian War for this conflict).

Antipater retreated with his surviving men into the city, which the Greeks then blockaded, cutting off its food supply to try to starve the enemy to death during the winter of 323–322. Demosthenes and Pytheas, both in exile from Athens, visited other Greek city-states to rally support—Demosthenes for the Greek side and Pytheas for the Macedonian. The ferocity of emotion aroused by the political divisions of this war burst into the open when the two men happened to be in the same Greek city at the same time to urge their respective causes. Alluding to the famous Greek medical expert Hippocrates' reports on donkey milk as an effective medicine for human ailments, Pytheas snidely remarked that in the same way that it was a sign of trouble to bring milk from a donkey into your house, so a city-state had to be sick to allow in an Athenian embassy. Demosthenes retorted that just as milk from a donkey can cure an illness, so too an Athenian embassy can rescue a city-state from its sufferings.[8]

And then the gods turned their backs on Athens. First, Leosthenes, the rebels' main commander, died from a blow to the head by a rock thrown during a skirmish outside Lamia's walls. As Hyperides said in the public funeral oration honoring the Athenians who died in this conflict, their general, though a hero fighting for Greek freedom, "could not escape fate." And now that same heartless divine power, as Greeks regarded it, descended on Athens itself. Antipater's reinforcements arrived in Greece from Asia in large numbers, led by Leonnatus, one of the chief Macedonian generals. These reinforcements compelled the Greek allies to end the siege of Lamia, freeing Antipater. Things became immeasurably worse when Athens's fleet of warships was out-admiraled in a battle on the Hellespont and then was defeated again off the island of Amorgos in the southern Aegean. The final disaster in the field came in August 322 near the town of Crannon in Thessaly, where the Macedonian phalanx crushed a valiant effort by tens of thousands of soldiers from the Greek allies. In the end, their commanders had to sue for peace to avoid total slaughter. Antipater took full advantage of this reversal of fortune by making deals with most of the allies, who accepted terms that fell short of devastation.[9]

CHAPTER TWELVE

Confronting Disaster and Revenge

B ut though he spared the Athenian army, Antipater had very different plans for Athens. He moved his commander's camp to the citadel of Thebes, amid its urban ruins, to prepare his army for an attack on Attica to the south. The Athenians panicked at the threat and passed a decree authorizing Phocion to go to Antipater to make peace for them, because, they said, Phocion was the only man they could trust. They presumably meant that the voters lacked confidence that their other leaders would forgo seeking personal profit while ostensibly negotiating a deal on the city-state's behalf. Phocion agreed to go, though only after dropping a typically aggressive response: "But if I had been trusted when giving you advice [about this war], we wouldn't now be figuring out what to do about conditions like these."[1]

When Phocion arrived at what was left of Thebes to meet with Antipater, he asked the victor to abstain from ravaging Athenian territory. Antipater's lieutenants strongly objected, but Antipater said, "We have to extend to Phocion this kindness." The old Macedonian apparently granted Phocion's request because he recognized the equally elder Athenian as a proponent of accommodation on the part of the Athenians. As for everything else, however, Antipater grimly demanded unconditional surrender. He said the Athenians had earned that treatment because it was the only option they had offered him when he and his troops were perishing of hunger during the siege of Lamia.[2]

Phocion returned to Athens bearing Antipater's dreadful ultimatum. The voters conceded to Antipater's demand out of what they saw as necessity (*ananke*) — a force that Greeks regarded as demonically divine. They sent Phocion back on an embassy to the Macedonian leader, accompanied by the philosopher Xenocrates of Chalcedon. Phocion knew Xenocrates personally because he was serving as the current leader of the Academy at Athens. The voters hoped Antipater would respect Xenocrates as a voice of wisdom in the tradition of Plato. They miscalculated badly. Antipater angrily reduced Xenocrates to silence by contradicting everything he said. As a Macedonian victor, Antipater resented the implication that any self-important Greek intellectual could tell him how to behave.

Antipater then gave Phocion his merciless terms for the Athenians: give up Demosthenes and Hyperides for punishment, restructure their government by restricting citizen rights on the basis of wealth, pay the costs of the war plus a fine, and accept a garrison to be stationed on the hill of Munychia overlooking the port of Piraeus. Phocion implored Antipater not to impose this garrison. His plea failed when he could give no answer when Antipater asked him whether he could guarantee that the Athenians would remain compliant if no garrison were installed. Phocion and the other ambassadors (with the exception of Xenocrates) then reluctantly agreed to the victor's terms for Athens. Xenocrates summed up the outcome of the mission by observing that Antipater had treated the Athenians with moderation if he regarded them as slaves, but crushingly if he considered them a free people. From the philosopher's point of view, Antipater's terms for Athens amounted to de facto enslavement.[3]

The horrifying reality of Xenocrates' assessment of the Athenians' situation became clear when a Macedonian garrison was installed on the nearly three-hundred-foot-tall Munychia Hill in Piraeus. This location gave the Macedonians effective control of the port. Their virtual imprisonment of Athens shocked the citizens beyond belief. The Athenians' dismay was heightened by the fact that the disaster took place on the twentieth day of the month of Boedromion, a hallowed date in the city-state's history. On that very day in 480, the Athenian fleet had stunned the world by routing the Persian navy at the Battle of Salamis off the western coast of Attica. The Great King had watched in dismay from atop a nearby hill and then returned home to Persia after his humiliating defeat. The day Boedromion 20, to offer a U.S. analogy, was the Athenians' Fourth of July, the linchpin of their treasured memory of an unexpected victory that preserved their freedom.

This earlier triumph, Athenians believed, had reflected the gods' devotion to their salvation because it occurred during the major religious ceremony commemorating the favor their homeland enjoyed from the goddess Demeter in her nearby sanctuary at Eleusis. And for Phocion, it was a horrible irony that his long-ago victory at Naxos, won at the same time of the year, had been commemorated by Chabrias's providing wine for this same celebration of Demeter's goodwill for the polis to whose safety he had devoted himself. In 322, by contrast with 480, the Athenians on Boedromion 20 had to conclude with horror that "the gods were now on this same sacred occasion overseeing the worst-ever sufferings of Greece . . . on a day that would become forevermore the date of their greatest calamities." In short, Phocion's contemporaries labeled this the worst day in the history of Athens.[4]

Their assessment seems comprehensible given Antipater's punishment of Athens. On the motion of Demades, the Assembly passed official sentences of death on Demosthenes and Hyperides, who had already fled the city upon the news that Antipater was on his way there. Their situation was hopeless. Demosthenes killed himself to escape capture, while Hyperides was dragged from a temple of the god Poseidon by a bounty hunter and killed. Antipater limited citizen rights in Athens to those who possessed two thousand drachmas of personal property. This harsh measure ended the Athenians' equality of citizenship and disenfranchised between twelve thousand and twenty-two thousand male citizens (the sources conflict). In either case, the number represented an overwhelming percentage of the adult male population. Furthermore, stipends were ended for holding public office, serving on juries, and attending the Assembly. These financial subsidies had previously enabled even poorer Athenians to take part in governing, but once their participation was no longer supported they lost their voice. The government was reduced to the service and votes of only nine thousand male Athenians.

The full and terrible consequences of Antipater's control became clear when he oversaw sending many (the total is uncertain) of the now disenfranchised Athenians to make a new life in Thrace, hundreds and hundreds of miles to the north. There these now homeless Greeks would become outsiders who could have no sense of belonging in their new environment. Phocion, realizing the depth of despair his contemporaries felt, prevailed upon Antipater to allow some of them to migrate instead to the Peloponnese. He even successfully intervened for this favor on behalf of Hagnonides, an orator notorious for bringing legal accusations and then accepting bribes to drop the charges. Thanks to Phocion, Hagnonides was allowed to take refuge in southern Greece rather than trek all the way to the far north. No information survives on why Phocion undertook this particular act of mercy, but it turned out to be one that he would regret.

Modern scholars have argued over how harsh an evaluation to offer concerning the dramatic alterations in Athenian life that Antipater engineered to keep Athens from threatening his ambitions to become the most powerful force in the eastern Mediterranean. They offer different views on whether to regard Athens's newly imposed political regime as a moderate democracy or an oligarchy, as well as on the nature of the mass immigration to Thrace. The scholars disagree on whether the new government ordered by Antipater destroyed Athenian democracy or reset it in a more stable form, and on whether the mass of people leaving Athens was being forcibly expelled or readily accepting a chance for a new start in a new land.[5] In my judgment, the harsher view – that Antipater was cruelly punishing Athens – is unavoidable when we recognize the emotional blow the people felt from their baffled sense of betrayal by their patron deities. Moreover, the crowds of former citizens leaving Athens would have had to endure immense physical and financial burdens, able to take with them only what they could carry on their exhausting and dangerous odyssey. They must have felt a crushing sense of loss.

Understanding their anguish also helps us grasp why feelings at Athens became so inflamed in the years following the conclusion of the Lamian War in 322. This was the period when Phocion, now in his eighties, would experience both the height of his public prominence and the nadir of his career. The length of Phocion's public service meant that by this date a substantial percentage of adult Athenians would have now been too young to have extensive personal memories of his valorous early career fighting for their polis. Even though his contemporary Athenians credited Phocion with some later successes, their current catastrophe would compel them to feel far too little emotional connection with him to dispel suspicions about his devotion to belonging to the demos.

Antipater for his part regarded Phocion as a steadying influence in postwar Athens. Perhaps the Macedonian regent thought the Athenians would respect Phocion for his great age, as Greek tradition prescribed. Regardless, Antipater left the drastically diminished institutions of Athenian government formally in place, and Phocion was not made dictator. However, his advice to the Assembly now carried the greatest weight because everyone knew that he had a direct line to the man holding ultimate power over them. To try to keep Athens calm and curry favor with Antipater, Phocion appears to have pushed the wealthiest and most educated of the nine thousand to serve in the new government's unpaid offices. He encouraged the poorer citizens who had not been expelled to concentrate on agricultural work. Xenocrates refused to acknowledge the propriety of these new arrangements. When Phocion offered to have Xenocrates honored with Athenian citizenship, the philosopher publicly turned him down on the grounds that he refused to be part of a political system whose creation he had tried to prevent.

Phocion at least did not alter his determination to stay unsullied by bribes intended by Athens's conquerors to influence his political stance. Most strikingly, he decided to stay on friendly terms with Menyllus, the commander of the Macedonian garrison, even after being offered money to become a collaborator. Phocion refused the cash on the grounds that Menyllus was not a better man than Alexander had been; Phocion had of course turned down that king's stupendous gift offer to him. Phocion apparently judged Menyllus to be reasonable and fair in the exercise of his power over the defeated Athenians — at least to the extent that opposing him would be detrimental to Athens's safety, such as it now was. So far as we can tell, Phocion was able to maintain a less than servile relationship with Menyllus for the next several years. And when Antipater himself tried to pressure Phocion into doing something (unspecified) that the Athenian saw as wrong, Phocion gave a typically pointed answer: "Antipater cannot make use of me simultaneously as a friend and as a flatterer." Antipater nevertheless left Phocion unharmed, no doubt calculating that Phocion's strict devotion to maintaining what he as an Athenian saw as his homeland's safety would also serve the Macedonians' interest.[6]

In short, Phocion's nominal oversight of civic policy during this period of suffering for the many of Athens meant that no overt resistance was offered to Antipater by the city-state's newly restricted alleged democracy. Phocion's most controversial decision in this tense situation was to reject time and time again pleas from his countrymen to try to persuade Antipater to remove the Macedonian garrison from Munychia. Menyllus's troops were not physically terrorizing the population, but Athenians realized that these occupiers could at any moment march out to close the port lying just below their hilltop fortress. In other words, the Macedonian garrison held a potential stranglehold on the city. Why Phocion refused to plead for the garrison's removal is a crucial question for whose answer the sources offer not even a hint. The only possible guess we can make is that he must have believed that enduring the omnipresent threat from foreign troops in their midst was the best guarantee of physical, though not emotional or political, safety for Athenians because it forestalled a revolution he thought could only culminate in further disaster for them. This was a momentous choice, for his personal fate above all.

The Athenians' continuing anguish led them in 319 to persuade the pro-Macedonian Demades to accept a mission to beg Antipater to end the garrison's hold on Athens. He set out for Macedonia accompanied by his son. But Antipater fell seriously ill around this time.

As his designated replacement, Antipater chose Polyperchon, who had served as a general under Philip and Alexander. With this surprising choice, Antipater dramatically passed over his own son Cassander, whom he demoted to second in line. In reality, whoever was serving as the caretaker of Philip III Arrhidaeus became the regent in Macedonia, and currently Polyperchon occupied that position. After Antipater died in the fall of 319, Cassander acted to promote himself as a leading competitor in the emerging struggle among prominent Macedonians to become the new Alexander.

These would-be Successors (as they are now designated) to what they hoped would be their personal revival of the power of Alexander the Great were besotted with ambition and violence. Cassander led the pack on that score among these first aspirants to Alexander's power. When Cassander discovered that Demades was actually in league with Antigonus One-Eye, one of the other Successors competing with him, Antipater's son immediately had the orator's son slaughtered while he stood beside his father so that his child's blood inundated Demades' cloak. The Macedonian then ignominiously berated the Athenian as a traitor before killing him as well. This incident suggests that Antipater may have passed Cassander over as the next ruler of the mainland Greeks because he recognized his son's propensity for inhumanely cruel behavior.

The rivalry of Cassander and Polyperchon soon erupted into an open hostility that engulfed Phocion. In this competition for dominance, Cassander snuck away from Macedonia, secretly heading for Asia Minor to seek support against Polyperchon from Antigonus One-Eye, who had served as a prominent older general under Alexander. Antigonus pretended to be in sympathy with Cassander, when in fact he was plotting his own attempt to become regent. In a move that would eventually seal Phocion's fate, Cassander dispatched his Macedonian lieutenant Nicanor to replace Menyllus as the commander of the garrison at Athens. Nicanor numbered among Cassander's "Companions," the traditional Macedonian designation for men of high status who enjoyed their leader's trust and confidence.

When the Athenians learned of Cassander's ploy to replace Menyllus and put his own agent in charge of the garrison, they became enraged at Phocion. They angrily blamed him for not letting them know of this change ahead of time. They believed that they had missed an opportunity to seize on a moment of apparent uncertainty for their Macedonian opponents and rise up to expel their foreign oppressors. In their rage, they accused Phocion of conspiring with Nicanor to become his ally. Phocion in response brusquely shrugged off their criticism, evidently confident that he could persuade Nicanor to show goodwill toward the Athenians. Perhaps Phocion thought that Nicanor's membership in the Macedonian social elite made him someone with whom he could do business, so to speak, even if, as an Athenian, Phocion was now in truth, like all his countrymen, at the mercy of this foreign commander. By conferring with the new garrison commander, Phocion did in fact persuade him to pay for some athletic competitions staged as public entertainment in Athens. This concession may well have fooled Phocion into thinking that he had been right to negotiate with Nicanor instead of seeking to organize armed Athenian resistance against his takeover of the garrison.

To grasp the full consequences of Phocion's extremely controversial decision to cooperate with the new devil, Nicanor, at this critical juncture, we must follow the doleful train of subsequent events as best the limited surviving sources allow. They show plainly that that decision proved to be Phocion's downfall. Discontent with Phocion at Athens worsened exponentially when Polyperchon announced a new policy deceptively attributed to King Philip III. The Greeks were granted a return to the governments they had possessed during the reigns of Philip II and Alexander; their exiles (with the exception of certain criminals) were permitted to return; and—revealing the truth behind the proclamation—they were ordered to demonstrate loyalty to Philip III by following the instructions of Polyperchon. For Athens, this revolutionary proclamation announced that the city-state's former democracy would be restored, the citizens disenfranchised by Antipater would regain their full citizen rights, and those expelled from Attica would return if Polyperchon could end Cassander's control—now being exercised by Nicanor—over Athens. Evaluating the sincerity of Polypherchon's words was impossible, but the Athenian many could only rejoice at the possibility, no matter how slight, that he meant what he said.

Polyperchon also wrote to Olympias, Alexander the Great's mother, to propose an alliance with her to block Cassander's ambitions. Since she resented the arrogance of Antipater's son as a diminution of her self-proclaimed status as the kingdom of Macedon's premier royal woman, Polyperchon easily convinced Olympias to side with him. He promised that she could take charge of Alexander's posthumous son Alexander IV, now about four years old, and raise him as king alongside Philip III. Polyperchon also planned to promote his own interests by undermining Phocion's influence in Athens. The Macedonian hoped thereby to secure the support of the large number of socially nonelite and now politically disempowered or even physically displaced Athenians in his conflict with Cassander over who was going to fill the power vacuum created by Alexander the Great's death.

The stars continued to align against Phocion when Nicanor publicly urged the Athenians to serve their best interests by siding with Cassander instead of Polyperchon. They indignantly responded that the garrison had to be removed. Saying that he needed time to bring this about, Nicanor secretly began adding more soldiers to his force on Munychia. Nicanor also asked to address the Athenians so he could warn them against trusting Polyperchon, and the Council of Five Hundred agreed to a meeting at Piraeus. Nicanor relied on Phocion to prevent violence against him on this highly fraught occasion, but Dercyllus, the Athenian general in charge of the Piraeus area, decided to try to capture the new garrison commander. When Nicanor succeeded in fleeing this attack, the people harshly castigated Phocion for letting their oppressor escape. His response was characteristically not designed to win him new friends — he said that he still had faith in Nicanor's good intentions and that in any case he, Phocion, would rather endure injustice than inflict it.

Events immediately revealed that Phocion's judgment of Nicanor's character was disastrously flawed. Just as had occurred thirty years earlier during his dealing with the tyrant on Euboea, Phocion was betrayed by someone whose surface appearance of cooperation had initially deceived him. Nicanor gathered a corps of mercenary soldiers to make a covert nighttime foray into the main section of Piraeus. The Macedonian's men seized the wall surrounding the port and the large boom that was raised and lowered to control the entry and exit of ships through the harbor's opening to the sea. Nicanor now had an unbreakable death grip on Athens's throat.

Belatedly acknowledging the threat to his city-state and Nicanor's betrayal of his trust, Phocion now offered to command the Athenians in an attack on their enemy. But he was too late in admitting his terrible mistake in evaluating the reality underlying Nicanor's promises. Phocion's fellow citizens mocked his abrupt change of mind and angrily rejected his leadership. Instead, they compelled him and two other political leaders, Conon and Clearchus, to approach Nicanor because they were thought to be on good terms with him. Their orders were to denounce Nicanor's actions to his face

and demand that the Macedonian obey the provisions of Polyperchon's decree by restoring Athens's democracy and freedom. Nicanor refused to answer the envoys directly, claiming that the Athenians' representatives needed to confer directly with Cassander—he,
Cassander's garrison commander, lacked the authority to authorize
such a change.

At this moment the Athenians learned that a letter had arrived
for Nicanor from Olympias, who regally ordered him to return control of Munychia and Piraeus to the citizens of Athens. Nicanor had
by now learned of Polyperchon's plan to elevate Alexander's mother
to a central role in the opposition to Cassander, and he evidently
worried that her popularity could ruin his leader's chances of seiz-
ing the throne for himself. So Nicanor deceptively promised the
Athenians that he would follow Olympias's mandate. Believing this
lie, the people praised the queen and rejoiced at what they thought
was the imminent recovery of their autonomy.

The Athenians were further heartened when the son of Polyperchon, also named Alexander, unexpectedly arrived in Attica in early
318 and encamped near Piraeus. They mistakenly believed this Alexander had come to put his father's decree for their liberation into
effect; in fact, he, too, had ulterior motives. He planned to seize
the port and the city to advance his own power while the Athenians
continued to render themselves impotent through their unhealable
divisions. Falling for these falsehoods, the Athenians who were
now rejecting Phocion proved that he had not been not alone in
making catastrophic errors of judgment when he failed to see beyond the appearances of the ambitious manipulators vying for dominance over Athens.

Alexander's arrival changed much more than the military balance at Athens because he brought along a huge cadre of Athenians
from among the exiles who had been so brutally disenfranchised

and expelled in 322. These returning exiles in turn had with them a large number of non-Athenians with whom they had made connections during their struggle to survive as homeless victims of political upheaval. These returnees were out for revenge. As emotions peaked, Phocion met secretly with Alexander, advising him to keep his hold on the strategic points in Attica until Cassander could be defeated and freedom restored to Athens. Phocion perhaps offered this compromise in part out of concern for his own safety in the face of the wrath of the returned citizens, but he also surely calculated that Cassander's documented viciousness made him the greatest threat to Athens's safety posed by the battling Successors.

The inescapable truth was that none of these would-be dynasts was trustworthy. Having to deal both with treacherous competitors for the Macedonian monarchy and a seething mass of returning exiles put Phocion on a fast path to destruction. A raucous Assembly meeting promptly convened, dominated by the furious and vengeful crowd. They summarily dismissed from office every man currently holding a government position and filled the vacancies with unshakeable proponents of direct democracy. The new officials refused any compromise with foreigners seeking to restrict their independence in setting domestic and foreign policy. The voters in this tempestuous meeting also decreed penalties for the citizens whom they condemned as collaborators. Some they sentenced to death, others they punished with exile and confiscation of all their property.

At this crucial moment, Hagnonides denounced Phocion as a traitor, probably because he was looking for a public reward as informer.

This was the same Hagnonides whom Phocion in 322 had rescued from exile in far-away Thrace. First Hagnonides the Athenian, now Nicanor the Macedonian – Phocion had badly misjudged them both, fatally as it would turn out. His mistakes in discerning the hidden characters of these men suggest that he was simply incapable of looking beyond the surface of people to recognize their true character. It seems inescapable that he harbored some sort of misplaced belief — or at least desperate hope — that other powerful individuals within the social elite would choose the path of dikaiosune, rectitude and justice, in dealing with him, the way he regarded himself as doing toward them.

Deprived of any other option in the face of Hagnonides' accusation of treason, Phocion managed to sneak out of town accompanied by a small cadre of faithful friends. One of them, Deinarchus, had been a close friend of Antipater. The group made its way to Polyperchon's camp in the region of Phocis, north of Athens. There they found that an Athenian embassy had also arrived to address the regent. These envoys delivered a decree of Hagnonides that the newly constituted Athenian Assembly had formerly approved, charging Phocion with capital crimes against his polis.

In a dramatically staged scene, Polyperchon seated himself and Philip III Arrhidaeus under a golden canopy to hear the competing pleas of the two groups. The moment Deinarchus started to speak, Polyperchon had him tortured and then executed. The facade of fairness in this impromptu court shattered in a shower of blood. The Athenians led by Hagnonides then tumultuously impugned Phocion. The uproar became so volcanic that Hagnonides shouted to Polyperchon, "Throw us all into a cage and ship us back to Athens to argue our cases!" Philip III, the ostensible judge of the proceedings, laughed out loud. When Phocion tried to defend himself, Polyperchon interrupted his every word, reducing him to a disgusted silence. The fake trial abruptly ended when Polyperchon shouted to one of Phocion's defenders, "Stop spouting lies about me in front of the king here!" Philip III in his habitual confusion promptly tried to spear the Athenian speaker who was urging Phocion's innocence. Polyperchon had to wrestle the impaired king away, putting an abrupt end to the farce of an impartial hearing.[7]

Phocion and his companions were promptly shipped off to Athens under guard, purportedly for a regular court appearance before their fellow citizens. But nothing was going to be regular about their treatment. Upon arrival, they were unceremoniously hauled in wagons through the streets to the main theater, where they were detained for all to stare at and mock before their trial. An Assembly meeting was called, and everyone was admitted without going through an identity check: citizen and foreigner, free and slave. A letter in the name of Philip III was read in which the king condemned the prisoners as traitors but left the final decision to the Athenians. When friends of Phocion protested that noncitizens in fairness ought to leave the Assembly, the crowd yelled that these speakers, too, should be stoned for treason because they were responsible for the slavery of the country and the dissolution of its direct democracy.

Phocion then asked how he could receive a fair trial if he was going to be shouted down whenever he tried to explain his actions. The audience in response became so loud that nothing could be heard above their furious words of abuse. Exasperated and devoid of hope, Phocion finally exclaimed, "I agree that I did wrong, and I give myself the death penalty for my political acts. But, men of Athens, why are you going to kill these men who are with me when they have done nothing wrong?" The crowd roared back, "Because they are your friends!" When Hagnonides proposed the conviction and execution of all the prisoners, the only concession made was to reject a proposal to torture them to death.[8]

As with the condemnation of a group of generals after the battle off the Arginusae Islands in 406/5, the entire process contravened Athens's long-established legal protocols for court trials. It was still the law that capital charges were required to be brought against individual defendants in separate trials, not against a group of defendants tried simultaneously. Moreover, jurors were supposed to be vetted as citizens in good standing. Now, in 318, Athens's legal protections were again abandoned. Phocion and the other defendants were convicted of treason when the defeats and anxieties of the times overwhelmed the Athenians, leading them to overrule their restored democracy's tradition of respecting established law to promote the well-being of everyone.

Phocion's friends lamented and cried alongside him as the convicted men were led away to the jail to be executed. Jurors and spectators from the trial followed the prisoners, bellowing insults. One man even ran up to spit in Phocion's face. Showing no emotion or upset, the condemned Phocion turned to his guards and asked, "Won't someone stop this plebeian?" At the jail, Phocion did his best to lead his fellow defendants in displaying no perturbation at their unjust fate. His best, as always, was expressed with a sharp edge. When one of the others angrily protested that it was unfitting for him to be executed with Phocion, the latter replied, "What, you don't love that you are going to die with Phocion?" But when a friend asked him if he had any last words for his son Phocus, Phocion, ever the protective though prescriptive father, cautioned, "I say not to hold it against the Athenians." Like Phocion's audience at the time, we are left to contemplate whether he offered this paternalistic command out of concern that his son might risk trouble by seeking vengeance. Perhaps with his unexpected words he meant to head off the danger of provoking yet more political division in Athens's fractured and fractious democracy. In any case, his reference to the Athenians strongly implies that here, at the very end, he still felt unable truly to belong to the community whose safety he had done his best to protect—but failed.[9]

Phocion was last in the lineup of condemned prisoners who were to drink the potion of pounded hemlock that as a powerful poison was sometimes used for carrying out the death penalty instead of strangulation. By the time the executioner got to Phocion, though, he had used up all the deadly doses he had prepared. This public servant then demanded twelve drachmas, the equivalent of two weeks' pay, to make up the final draught. Wryly commenting that in Athens not even dying came gratis, Phocion asked a friend to pay the executioner the cash. The execution, in the late spring of 318, fell on a day when Athens held a sacred procession in honor of Zeus led by men on horseback. Holding a public execution at the time of an official ceremony honoring the gods was a remarkable departure from tradition. (By contrast, the execution of Socrates had been delayed for a number of days to avoid overlapping with a religious occasion.) That this tradition was disregarded in Phocion's case points to the depth of hatred the majority of citizens felt for him.

Disgrace was then added to Phocion's annihilation when the Athenians who had detested him convinced the Assembly to vote to have the executed men's bodies carried beyond the borders of Attica and abandoned there without a funeral service. Depriving cadavers of the traditional rites of burial or cremation was an extreme gesture of contempt and anger on the part of the political power holders in a Greek community. Phocion's friends decided not to risk defying this order, so they hired a funeral worker to take his body across the boundary between Athens and Megara to the west and then surreptitiously kindle a fire there for cremation. Phocion's wife showed herself truly courageous by taking her maidservants to the spot to construct a memorial and pour libations on the ground. Before leaving to return to Athens by night, she hid the bones of Phocion's charred remains in the fold of her gown to sneak them home to bury in their hearth. She privately commemorated her spouse's memory by saying as she interred them, "To you, beloved hearth, I give over these remains from a good man; return them to his ancestral tombs whenever the Athenians will be sound of mind."[10]

CHAPTER THIRTEEN

The Memory of Phocion, Then, Later, Now

The wishes of Phocion's wife for Athens's well-being came true in some ways. When yet another drastic change in the city-state's governance occurred soon after her husband's death, the official Athenian memory of Phocion underwent a complete and positive refashioning. And much later, beginning in early modern times, his image was revived as a point of reference in political disagreements between proponents of authoritarian regimes and those of democracies. The debate over Phocion's reputation also continues in modern scholarly studies. And today, trends in U.S. politics emphasize the relevance of thinking about what his life story might have to tell us concerning contemporary dangers to democracy.

Following Phocion's death in 318, the aspiring Successors Cassander, Polyperchon, and Antigonus continued to struggle among themselves for power. Neither they nor any of the other pretenders to Alexander's legacy ever fully succeeded in gaining unrivaled power, and his conquests were ultimately divided among various of his lieutenants. In modern terminology, this point marked the transition from the Classical Age of ancient Greek history to the Hellenistic Age. In mainland Greece, Cassander and Polyperchon were the main contenders for dominance. They initially fought at Athens, but Cassander won the final prize when forces loyal to him foiled Polyperchon's siege of Megalopolis in the Peloponnese in 317. This humiliating setback for Polyperchon motivated a number of Greek communities to declare their allegiance to Cassander. Among them was Athens. At a highly contentious debate in the Assembly, the voters finally but unanimously decided that to ensure their survival they had to seek the best deal that they could get from Cassander. This calculated, if regrettable, decision based on a harsh reality in international affairs was the same kind of difficult choice that Phocion had consistently advocated throughout his career.

Cassander's terms were a combination of concession and repression. The Athenians would keep their territory, their public revenues, and their fleet, but Cassander would retain a garrison on Munychia until the war with his rivals ended. This was a false promise, as he intended to keep permanently his garrison's hold on the Athenians' main port and therefore on their food supply chain. The only citizens permitted to be active in Athenian government were those who possessed property valued at one thousand drachmas. This was half the amount that Antipater had imposed in 322 at the end of the Lamian War, probably reflecting the financial stresses Athens's population had continued to experience since that disaster. Most significant, Cassander would pick an Athenian citizen to be the city-state's overseer or governor (*epimeletes*). This was a euphemism for a sole ruler. In 317 he chose Demetrius of Phaleron (a smaller port of Athens near Piraeus). Demetrius presided (ruled) over Athens for ten years, until he was expelled by the Macedonian Successor Demetrius the Besieger, son of Antigonus One-Eye. Despite future periods of relative independence, the Athenians would never again regain the power and glory, or the unrestricted democracy, that in their patriotic memories they attributed to the ancestors who had repulsed the Persians in the fifth century. In the long run, Athens, like the rest of Greece, ended up under Roman control.

The opening years of the regime of Demetrius of Phaleron did, however, see a dramatic change in how Phocion was remembered, at least officially. Demetrius reengineered Phocion's reputation, declaring him a national hero. A bronze statue commemorating Phocion was erected in downtown Athens, and his bones were retrieved from their hidden burial at his home and honored with a public funeral. The message was clear: the mob driving Athenian democracy before Cassander's reform had made a grievous, if characteristic, error in condemning and disgracing this useful and good Athenian. The Assembly heard the message and condemned Hagnonides to death, reflecting Demetrius's suggestion that Phocion's countrymen demonstrate that they rejected demagoguery. They should, Demetrius made clear, recognize the need to follow the political lead of socially elite leaders. What everyone understood by this was that these upper-class citizens were cloaking their iron hands in the velvet gloves of a democracy now allegedly restored to its ancestral purity. Phocion's son Phocus tracked down two of his father's enemies to take revenge on them. Characteristically, our ancient sources reveal nothing to help us solve the puzzle of what could have been his genuine motives in light of his notoriously troubled relationship with Phocion. All we know is that Phocion's son ultimately took dramatic action to honor his father's memory.

The later memory of Phocion has its own striking history. His career never generated a high level of interest among Greek and Roman writers after his time, as my brief survey of the ancient sources shows. Frankly, Phocion might well have sunk into near total obscurity, like so many other notable figures from antiquity, if it had not been for the intense popularity that Plutarch's works achieved in early modern Europe and Britain. The sixteenth-century scholar and churchman Jean-Jacques Amyot devoted himself to translating Greek literature into French, and in midlife he went to Italy to access a manuscript of Plutarch's biographies owned by the Vatican. In 1559 Amyot produced a printed translation of Plutarch's *Parallel Lives* in French titled *Les Vies des hommes illustres des Grecs et Romains* (The Lives of Famous Men of the Greeks and Romans). This book became highly influential, providing access to these texts to readers who could not read ancient Greek.

As mentioned at the start of this book, Plutarch explicitly stressed that in his biographies he was investigating not history but rather the character of significant leaders from Greek and Roman antiquity as they wrestled with personal challenges in an effort to lead influential lives. Plutarch's pairing of a Greek life with a Roman life opened the way for readers to contemplate how different cultural and historical environments could affect the moral successes and failures of famous figures from the European past. This comparative ethical tack, to say nothing of the frequently fascinating anecdotes and quotations Plutarch included, attracted many readers in Amyot's time.

One of those was Sir Thomas North, who in 1579 published his English translation of Plutarch's biographies, *The Lives of the Noble Grecians and Romanes Compared*. He based his translation on Amyot's French text instead of the original Greek, and the word *Noble* in his title reflected the moral interests that intrigued readers new to Plutarch. North's work became very influential in spreading knowledge of Plutarch's biographies to readers of English. William Shakespeare, for example, used North's translation as a source for plays that he wrote with settings from ancient history, though Phocion did not become one of the playwright's subjects.

Artists took inspiration from Phocion's story as told by Plutarch to paint images implicitly expressing the injustice of his treatment by the many. In 1648, the French painter Nicolas Poussin produced two scenes focused on Phocion's posthumous fate, *The Funeral of Phocion* and *The Ashes of Phocion Collected by His Widow*. These were landscapes, whose depictions of ancient architecture framing the exposure of Phocion's remains contextualize the dead Athenian as a tragic hero scorned by his own community.

Poussin was clearly familiar with Plutarch's biographies, for he also painted scenes related to Cato, whose life Plutarch paired with that of Phocion. The serenity of Poussin's scenes showing Phocion's body being carried out of Athens and his wife gathering up the burned traces of his cremation dramatically contrast with the violence and emotion that led up to these moments of calm. As for representations of Phocion himself, he appeared in paintings showing him remaining unperturbed at the site of his execution. For example, an 1804 painting by the Belgian artist Joseph Denis Odevaere shows Phocion at the moment when he and the friends who had been convicted of treason are taking poison as their death penalty. While the friends weep and wail as they die, Phocion sits amid them stoically, like a philosopher in the style of Socrates as described by Plato. Odevaere and others who painted Phocion's death scene thus depicted Phocion as a second Socrates, who himself was commemorated in paintings in the same manner. Jacques-Louis David, for example, in 1766 portrayed Socrates seated in complete composure at the site of his execution despite the agitated emotional state of the companions surrounding him.

In the eighteenth century, Plutarch's Phocion became an explicitly political figure of reference. The philosopher, historian, and political theorist Gabriel Bonnet de Mably (Abbé de Mably) published his *Entretiens de Phocion* (Conversations of Phocion) in 1763.

Scholars disagree about whether Mably's thought was proto-communist, moderately revolutionary, or classically republican, but this fictional work clearly derived its melancholy tone from the ending of Plutarch's biography. After describing Phocion in a series of conversations about the complex and confusing intertwining of politics and moral rectitude, Mably's imaginative scenario climaxed with a tearful Phocion rejecting violence as the way to protect Athens's freedom. He instead reluctantly advised his contemporaries to bend themselves to the unwelcome effects of the unsettling vicissitudes imposed on them by fortune, in this case the oppressive dominance of the Macedonian Successors.

Phocion appeared across the Atlantic transmuted into a contemporary political icon at the time of the American Revolution. As I noted in Chapter 1, in early 1784 Alexander Hamilton published a treatise titled *A Letter from Phocion to the Considerate Citizens of New York*. Later in the same year he penned a second "Phocion Letter" as a response to criticism of the first one. Hamilton used these tracts to argue for a Federalist view of structuring the U.S. government, in which the states would play a secondary role under a strong centralized administration. He also lamented the hostile treatment that was being meted out to the colonists who had supported the British side. Hamilton presumably chose "Phocion" as a pseudonym to show his support for a type of government that would rein in the untrammeled excesses of the mob.

Another active Federalist politician, the South Carolina congressman William Loughton Smith, also resurrected "Phocion" as a pseudonym for a series of twenty-five letters that were published in 1796. Smith's "Phocion" launched a series of attacks specifically directed at Thomas Jefferson's candidacy for the presidency. Presaging the bitter vitriol of today's political campaign pronouncements in the United States, Smith used Phocion's persona to blast Jefferson on a wide range of charges, including being a closet supporter of the violent masses involved in the French Revolution and deceptively untrustworthy in his views on the emancipation of slaves.

The use of Phocion as a symbol of a thoughtful elite whose approach to politics should supersede the passions of "the many" continued in European circles in the nineteenth century. The German philologist Jacob Bernays, for example, produced in 1881 a monograph that focused on the reception of Phocion beginning in the eighteenth century. His *Phokion und seine neueren Beurtheiler. Ein Beitrag zur Geschichte der griechischen Philosophie und Politik* (Phocion and His Recent Critics: A Contribution to the History of Greek Philosophy and Politics) approached Phocion as a philosopher who thought that direct democracy impeded a philosophical approach to just government. Bernays presented Phocion as favoring more high-minded and less free regimes as necessary for the success and survival of human communities.

In the mid-twentieth century, Phocion's life story inspired a book-length biography in French written by André Thérive. Published in 1948 soon after World War II, his *Vie de Phocion* (Life of Phocion) was a political treatise in the form of a biography meant to rebut Thérive's own contested reputation as a traitor. Thérive had served with distinction in World War I, being wounded twice and decorated for heroism. Over his career as a writer and literary critic, however, he developed a strong ethical aversion to what he regarded as political militarism. During World War II, he cooperated with the Vichy government, at least to the extent of serving on a board set up to regulate the scarce supply of paper for printing. After the war, he was accused of collaborating with the Nazis and publicly vilified.

Thérive composed his story of Phocion's fate under a pseudonym, Candidus d'Isaurie. Candidus of Isauria had been an imperial official and historian working in the eastern Roman Empire in the fifth century CE during a turbulent time when issues of political loyalty were being hotly contested. Thérive chose Phocion's story to demonstrate how a man driven by a philosophically resolute sense of integrity could be unjustly persecuted by his contemporaries on a charge of treason, which the Frenchman saw as his own equally and desperately unfair fate as well.

Scholars studying Phocion in the later twentieth century focus to a large extent on analyzing the reliability of the fragmentary surviving evidence concerning his life and emphasizing that the best documented period of that life by far encompasses only his final years. They disagree in their ultimate evaluations of how to characterize Phocion, as a person and as a leader. Hans-Joachim Gehrke in *Phokion. Studien zur Erfassung seiner historischen Gestalt* (Phocion: Studies on the Fashioning of His Historical Image, 1976) concludes that Phocion was correct in not supporting military action by Athens against Antipater after the Lamian War, and moreover that Phocion actually approved of the punishing restrictions imposed on his city-state in the war's aftermath. Cinzia Bearzot in *Focione tra storia e trasfigurazione ideale* (Phocion Between History and Idealizing Transfiguration, 1985) rejects much of the evidence portraying Phocion as an effective military and political leader and criticizes the tendency to turn him into a historical example of a philosopher in politics.

Lawrence A. Tritle's *Phocion the Good* (1988) is the scholarly book that with good reason is most often cited today. Tritle convincingly argues that Phocion was indeed successful in his military career overall, but he also aptly suggests that Phocion's brusque public manner harmed his ability to swing Athenian policy in the directions that as a patriotic Athenian he saw serving his homeland's best interests in times of crisis. In his conclusion, Tritle argues that Phocion's interaction with Plato gave him an intellectual depth of commitment to justice that made him a philosopher in politics.

Phocion thus on one hand seems to have intended to live his life as a useful and good citizen to his homeland and not to exploit his official position for personal profit. On the other, he never managed to convey to the majority of his contemporaries a compelling sense of belonging with them that would have convinced them to listen to his advice as coming from a friend. Perhaps worst of all, at the end of life, he clearly went wrong in his evaluations of other people at critical moments. His trusting the Macedonian garrison commander Nicanor was disastrous. Ultimately, Phocion's personal tragedy clearly had its deepest foundation in his inability to persuade his fellow citizens at this moment of crisis that they should heed his guidance and accept the distressing restrictions on their democratic freedom that he saw as necessary to secure their safety. So complete was his failure to convince the overwhelming majority that he was truly useful and good to them that he was executed and disgraced as a traitor.

The orator Hyperides in a speech from the late 330s defending another Athenian against a charge of treason gave a three-point definition of a useful and good citizen: he cares about the things that are "beneficial" to the polis over the long run, he cares about the "concord of feelings" among its citizens, and he cares about their "reputation." Phocion certainly cared deeply about the first point; this made him in his own mind a sincere patriot and therefore useful and good. The second and third points proved much more problematic in his case. His often aggressively barbed style of communicating about important policy issues did the opposite of encouraging harmony with other citizens who were equally interested in, but differently disposed regarding, what Athens should do. His comments tended to be exclusionary, either explicitly or implicitly making clear that he did not see himself as belonging to the people. In addition, his choice to live a publicly idiosyncratic personal life and to send his son to Sparta for his education did nothing to encourage solidarity with people who took his behavior as an implicit rejection of their more conventional habits. In this way, his personal behavior also distanced him from the communal sense of belonging that was so pronounced in Athenian culture.[1]

One inescapable conclusion is that Phocion failed to understand the critical need for political leaders in a democracy to forge positive emotional connections with the people whom they want to persuade to follow their recommendations. As history reveals, without some form of a sense of belonging together, there is no reasonable chance of persuading others to agree to a cooperative politics. The philosopher and polymath Aristotle was not himself an Athenian but he taught in his own school in Athens, the Lyceum, loosely modeled on Plato's Academy, from about 335 to 322 BCE. In his discussions of rhetoric and politics, Aristotle emphasized the central importance of leaders learning effective techniques of persuasion. In this context, Aristotle stressed that leaders needed to be able to appeal to people's emotions, by which he meant *pathos,* the feeling aroused by experiences that deeply affect people. Specifically, Aristotle explained, a persuasive speaker needs to begin a speech by focusing on these emotions stemming from experience.

Aristotle also makes clear that if a speaker wants to get his (and Aristotle has men in mind) listeners on his side, he will explain how his *ethos,* character based on habitual behavior, overlaps with the character of his audience. The speaker needs to convince his listeners that they share similar emotions about the issue under discussion and possess a character able to partake in cooperation for their shared advantage and benefit. In sum, the speaker will emphasize a sense of belonging to one another in a community that they all value. Given the stress in Athens on inculcating in males from a very young age a special sense of belonging and its concomitant set of responsibilities for them as citizens, an audience in the Assembly or councils or courts or military service at Athens would have been keenly receptive to this technique of persuasion — and deeply offended if they concluded that a fellow citizen was going out of his way to minimize his belonging to the people whom this ancestral notion defined.

It seems necessary to conclude that Phocion never fully appreciated or accepted Aristotle's crucial insight. There is no evidence that Phocion had any close association with Aristotle or his teachings, and Phocion certainly adopted as his own rhetorical style the more confrontational approach that Socrates used in private. Phocion's choice meant that his commitments to being useful and good and to keeping Athens safe were fatally undermined by his resolute rejection of any attempt to make himself more persuasive to others by expressing a sense of belonging with those whom he clearly felt capable of guiding. His distinctive mode of expressing himself led many others in Athens to conclude that he felt an emotion of *not* belonging with them and therefore induced them to lose faith in the genuineness of his wanting to be useful and good to his homeland.

Among the issues I have raised about the mystery of Phocion's condemnation and disgrace as a traitor to the homeland to which he devoted himself, one particular query related to his career and eventual fate and that of his democratic city-state seems important to ask because it is relevant for U.S. citizens to ponder today. As they struggle to find their nation's way forward in the midst of a furiously divided political and social environment, Americans might ask themselves, What should being a useful and good citizen and political leader mean here and now at a time when some in the United States are calling for a national divorce?

Phocion

To end with antiquity, however, it seems that Phocion ultimately failed so dramatically because he most often dealt with other people as abstractions, not as human beings with deeply felt emotions. As I have noted more than once, his personal and seemingly idiosyncratic notion of rectitude and justice, of being useful and good, kept him from experiencing a full sense of belonging with the Athenians as "the people." Evidently, he lacked the imagination to empathize with the emotions, the goals and fears, of the citizens whom he saw as the many, to see beyond surface appearances and class prejudices and grasp others' underlying realities. He often denigrated poorer Athenians, to judge from the many quotations in Plutarch's biography. But Phocion also shunned symposiums and dressed differently from other members of Athens's elite — a signal that he set himself apart from the social stratum into which he had been born. He simply found it impossible to connect with anyone in public, so far as we can tell, except perhaps the senior military comrades alongside whom he went into battle. Near the start of his biography Plutarch hints at this shortcoming in dealing with people in his homeland. Phocion's fellow Athenians, the biographer reports, "rarely saw him laughing or crying."[2]

Plutarch himself, in a philosophical essay on how to be an effective leader in which he refers to Phocion, expressed a view that may well have been at least in part influenced by what the biographer could see as a baneful result of Phocion's irascibility toward others. To be successful, Plutarch explained, a useful and good man must not "walk among the citizens with a look bitter for them to behold" but should be "easy to speak to and commonly available to everyone to approach." In a society like that of ancient Athens, which regarded displays of emotion and passion as the norm for human communication, the publicly cold and standoffish Phocion must have seemed to others around him to be consciously and deliberately setting himself apart from the society to which he was supposed to belong.[3]

The fundamental issue here is surely that Phocion's genuine concern for his polis was overwhelmingly abstract, an idea of a community instead of a grittily realistic assessment of the situation on the ground, so to speak. Although he saw his fellow citizens' safety as the ultimate criterion for policy decisions, he never succeeded in unlocking the mystery of how to summon the imagination required to create the emotional sense of belonging with other people that would have given him the best chance of persuading them to agree with him about how to secure their communal safety. In contemplating the life of Phocion as something that is good to think with concerning how U.S. democracy can be supported and preserved in a time of increasingly marked divisions, it seems fitting to end by quoting Adam Smith. He opens his *Theory of Moral Sentiments* (1759) with a thought-provoking description (expressed in the gendered language of the time) of the crucial type of emotional imagination that would have helped Phocion—and would help anyone anywhere anytime in truly being useful and good: namely, develop a personal sense of belonging with others that is aimed at reducing the suffering and increasing the safety of us all in a dangerous world: "As we have no immediate experience of what other men feel, we can form no idea of the manner in which they are affected, but by conceiving what we ourselves should feel in the life situation. Though our brother is upon the rack, as long as we ourselves are at our ease, our senses will never inform us of what he suffers. They never did and never can carry us beyond our own person, and it is by the imagination only that we can form any conception of what are his sensations."[4]

Chronology

All dates BCE.

490–479	Persian Wars, invasions of Greece by forces of the Persian king and his Greek subjects
480	Athenian-led victory over the Persian fleet at Salamis
451	Periclean Citizenship Law passed: only children of both an Athenian mother and an Athenian father in legitimate marriage can be citizens
431	Peloponnesian War between Athens and its allies and Sparta and its allies begins
406/5	Eight Athenian generals tried for failure in a sea battle and condemned to death at Athens; the six who show up for trial are executed
404	Athenians lose the Peloponnesian War; Spartans impose a garrison and oligarchic government by the Thirty Tyrants
403	Civil war in Athens overthrows Spartan-backed oligarchy and restores democracy
ca. 402	Birth of Phocion in Athens
399	Socrates tried and executed for impiety and corrupting Athens's youth
397	The Persian Great King Artaxerxes II builds a fleet to confront Spartan forces in Asia Minor
395–387	Corinthian War between pro-Spartan and anti-Spartan Greek city-states
394	Athenian commander Conon shares command of a Persian fleet to defeat the Spartans in a sea battle off Cnidos
386	King's Peace imposed by Artaxerxes II on Greek city-states with Spartan support
Mid-380s	Phocion becomes a student at the Academy of Plato
382	Spartans impose a garrison on the Thebans
379/8	Thebans expel the Spartan garrison
378	Spartans attack Thebes and are defeated by Chabrias, an Athenian general and mentor of Phocion

Chronology

378/7   Athenians create a naval alliance of Greek city-states (Second Athenian League)

376   Phocion wins glory as a trireme commander in a sea battle off the island of Naxos

373   Thebans take and raze the Boeotian city-state Plataea

371   Spartans invade Theban territory and are defeated at Leuctra

369   Athenians and Thebans ally against the Spartans

366   Phocion creates controversy with his advice on the military campaign at Oropos

362   Athenians, Spartans, and their allies fight the Thebans and their allies at Mantinea; the Thebans win but the aftermath is inconclusive

ca. 361   Phocion serves as a military commander when Athenians support the Satraps' Revolt against Artaxerxes II

359   Philip, son of the Macedonian king Amyntas III, rallies his countrymen to repulse an invasion from the north and soon becomes King Philip II of Macedon

357–355   Athens defeated in the Social War against rebel members of the Second Athenian League

351/0   Phocion serves on Cyprus as a mercenary military commander supporting Artaxerxes III, the Persian king

348   Phocion sent as a military commander to fight at the city-state of Eretria on the island of Euboea; Athenians send ineffectual military aid to Olynthus against Philip

346   Peace of Philocrates between Athens and Philip

343   Phocion leads Athenian military support for the neighboring city-state of Megara against Philip; defends Aeschines against Demosthenes in a court case

341   Phocion commands a force expelling a tyrant and restoring democracy to Eretria

340–338   Phocion serves as a general against Philip in northern Greece until he is wounded

338   Athens, Thebes, and other Greek city-states are defeated by Philip and his allies at the battle of Chaeronea

336   Philip forms the League of Corinth with Greek city-states to attack Persia; he is assassinated and his son Alexander (later Alexander the Great) becomes king

Chronology

335	Alexander attacks and destroys Thebes for rebelling against the League of Corinth
334	Alexander leads the combined Macedonian and League of Corinth armies to attack Persia
331	Sparta's small-scale rebellion against Alexander in the Peloponnese peninsula fails
324	Alexander's former treasurer Harpalus corrupts Athenian politicians with money stolen from Alexander's plunder; Alexander issues the Exiles Decree restoring Greeks banned from their home city-states; Alexander announces his deification
323	Alexander dies in Babylon
323–322	Athens joins other Greeks in the Lamian War against the Macedonian regent Antipater
322	Antipater defeats Athens and imposes drastic punishments, including restricted government and mass exiles; Phocion is recognized as the leading adviser for Athens's international relations
319	Antipater dies; other Macedonians fight to become Alexander's successor (Successor Wars)
318	Phocion is tried for treason and executed when exiled Athenians return home during the struggle among Macedonian would-be Successors to Alexander
317	Demetrius of Phaleron is made sole ruler of Athens by the Macedonian successor Cassander; he hails Phocion as a hero

Source Notes

For the benefit of readers, I have included currently available English translations of ancient works in the bibliography, but unless otherwise indicated, all translations of these works cited in the book are my own.

As I noted in Chapter 1, the surviving ancient sources for Phocion's biography are few and far between. This situation is especially challenging for reconstructing his life because the extant sources, such as they are, focus to an extreme degree on the astonishing, horrifying, and controversial events of the final years of his life (322–318 BCE), when, in his early eighties, he was still deeply involved in public affairs at Athens.

Fortunately, the surviving sources do make for captivating reading, though they do not always agree on what Phocion did or said. Readers are encouraged to turn to the extant versions of these vivid accounts because directly encountering the colorful Greek and Roman authors who offer their own far from neutral assessments of their subject is well worth the effort. Their admittedly limited accounts nevertheless do make it clear that we, like they, have much to think about in contemplating the lessons Phocion's character and actions have to offer about morality, politics, and society. The following survey of the ancient sources proceeds in the chronological order of their composition.

An idiosyncratically composed survey of Greek history in the first half of Phocion's life is preserved in an ancient historical work by his fellow Athenian Xenophon (ca. 430–350 BCE) titled *Hellenika* (Greek Things). Inexplicably, Xenophon in his narrative of this eventful period nowhere mentions Phocion himself.

Further contemporary evidence for the history of Phocion's era comes from fourth-century BCE public inscriptions and the texts of a variety of political orations. These documents provide helpful, and sometimes bluntly vitriolic, insights into the troubles and discords of public life in Phocion's Athens, as revealed by the collection of translated evidence in Phillip Harding, *From the End of the Peloponnesian War to the Battle of Ipsus*.

From much later times come, first, the surviving portions of the book *Library of History* (or simply *Library*) composed by the Greek historian Diodorus of Sicily, who wrote during the time of the violent political convulsions that ended the Roman Republic in the first century BCE. Diodorus describes a small number of episodes from Phocion's life, going into detail only about the catastrophic events that led to his execution. Diodorus blames what he labels the Athenian mob for angrily condemning Phocion.

From the pen of the first-century BCE Roman author Cornelius Nepos, we have a short but provocative biography of Phocion as one entry in Cornelius Nepos's collection *The Book on the Great Generals of Foreign Nations*. Nepos recognizes the integrity with which Phocion lived his life but blames him for his actions after the Lamian War following the death of Alexander the Great. There are scattered, very brief references relevant to Phocion in some other Roman-era sources such as Valerius Maximus (first century CE) in his collection of anecdotes called *Memorable Doings and Sayings,* and in the later Roman biographer Diogenes Laertius's *Lives of Eminent Philosophers*.

By far the best known and most influential—and in significant ways most frustrating—source that we have for Phocion's life was composed in probably the early second century CE by Plutarch. By Plutarch's lifetime half a millennium after Phocion's death, Greece had long been part of the extended imperial realm that the Romans created in the lands surrounding the Mediterranean Sea. Plutarch included his Life of Phocion in his still famous *Parallel Lives*. The title refers to Plutarch's arrangement in this work of the biographies of the men he includes (he offers no lives of women). He pairs the biography of a prominent man from Greek history with that of a prominent Roman. Plutarch links his biographies so that he can make comparisons between the two subjects' characters and their fates. His authorial goal is to provide lessons for his readers, especially on the topics of personal character, morality, and public leadership. Plutarch matches Phocion with Cato the Younger, the controversial conservative Roman politician whose life ended in suicide during the bitter political conflicts of the Roman civil war in the later first century BCE.

Plutarch explicitly states (Life of Alexander the Great, section 1) that he composed his *Lives* to reveal his subjects' characters in action and not to provide detailed historical surveys of all, or sometimes even very many, of the major military and political events in their lifetimes. In none of his biographies is this manifesto more valid than in the Life of Phocion. Plutarch pays more attention to reporting scores of the sharply biting comments that Phocion often made in politically and socially charged contexts than to setting out the narrative of important events of Athenian history in Phocion's time, whether domestic or international in nature. Plutarch in fact includes some sixty quotations of Phocion's often startlingly confrontational public remarks. Only in Plutarch's description of Phocion's tumultuous and ultimately disastrous final years does the biographer provide us with enough detail to help us grasp how things could have gone so horribly wrong for Phocion and for Athens. Even for these most discussed events in Phocion's life, however, Plutarch's descriptions and interpretations can diverge from those found in other ancient sources.

Notes

CHAPTER 1. PHOCION AND THE RUIN OF ATHENIAN DEMOCRACY

1. Plutarch, "Rules for Politicians," *Moralia* 823A. Croesus was a sixth-century BCE king of Lydia who was best remembered for his vast wealth.

2. Plutarch, Life of Phocion 9.

3. Plutarch, Life of Phocion 1.

4. Lévi-Strauss, *Le Totémisme*.

CHAPTER 2. DISCOVERING A DANGEROUS WORLD

1. Plato, *Timaeus* 26b.

2. Idomeneus cited in Plutarch, Life of Phocion 4; Cornelius Nepos, *The Book on the Great Generals* 19.1; Plutarch, Life of Phocion 4.

3. Golden, *Children and Childhood in Classical Athens*, 71, estimates the infant mortality rate as 25 to 35 percent; Beaumont, *Childhood in Ancient Athens*, 87, suggests it was up to 50 percent; Euripides, *Medea*, lines 250–251.

4. Plato, *Laws* 11.927d.

5. Isaeus, *Oration* 2.13.

CHAPTER 3. MEETING EXPECTATIONS AS A TEENAGE BOY

1. Aristotle, *Eudemian Ethics* 9.7.

2. Aeschines, *Oration* 3.78.

CHAPTER 4. TRAINING FOR THE MILITARY

1. Rhodes and Osborne, *Greek Historical Inscriptions*, 440–441.

2. Demosthenes, *Oration* 20.31.

CHAPTER 5. LEARNING ABOUT ATHENIAN DEMOCRACY

1. Plutarch, Life of Phocion 8, 9; Valerius Maximus, *Memorable Doings and Sayings* 3.8.2.

2. Diogenes Laertius, *Lives of Eminent Philosophers* 3.28 (following fragment 6).

3. Aelian, *Historical Miscellany* 2.16.

CHAPTER 6. STARTING A PUBLIC CAREER

1. Xenophon, *Hellenika* 2.2.23.

2. Isocrates, *Oration* 4.174.

3. Rhodes and Osborne, *Greek Historical Inscriptions,* 92–99.

CHAPTER 7. WINNING GLORY AS A YOUNG NAVAL COMMANDER

1. Demosthenes, *Oration* 50.11.

2. Demosthenes, *Oration* 8.24.29; Lysias, *Oration* 19.50.

3. See Schwenk, "Athens"; Sealey, *Demosthenes and His Time;* and Ober, *Political Dissent in Democratic Athens* for a spectrum of approaches in analyzing the situation.

4. The stone is now in the Epigraphic Museum in Athens, no. 10393. A photo appears in Gabrielsen, "The Navies of Classical Athens and Hellenistic Rhodes," p. 76, fig. 1.

5. Plutarch, Life of Phocion 6.

CHAPTER 8. FACING MIDLIFE CHALLENGES

1. Isocrates, *Oration* 14.5.

2. Plutarch, Life of Phocion 9.

3. Diogenes Laertius, *Lives of Eminent Philosophers* 3.24, cites this remarkable instance of Plato taking an active part in a controversial episode of Athenian public life.

4. Xenophon, *Hellenika* 7.5.27.

5. Plutarch, Life of Phocion 20, 30.

6. Plutarch, Life of Phocion 9.

7. On curse tablets, see Lamont, "Athenian Curse Practice," which mentions Phocion.

CHAPTER 9. DEALING WITH MACEDON

1. Isocrates, *Oration* 7.21–22.

2. Demosthenes, *Oration* 9.31.

3. Isocrates, *Oration* 8.64, 142.

4. Plutarch, Life of Phocion 12.

5. Plutarch, Life of Phocion 13.

6. Demosthenes, *Oration* 5.5.

7. Aeschines, *Oration* 2.184.

8. Plutarch, Life of Phocion 9.

CHAPTER 10. ENDURING A CATASTROPHE

1. Plutarch, Life of Phocion 14.

2. Demosthenes, *On the Crown* 18.172–179.

3. Plutarch, Life of Phocion 16.

4. Lycurgus, *Against Leocrates* 50.

5. Plutarch, Life of Phocion 5.

6. Plutarch, Life of Phocion 16.

7. Diodorus, *Library of History* 16.87.1–2

8. Cornelius Nepos, *The Book on the Great Generals* 19.1.

9. Plutarch, Life of Phocion 16.

10. Plutarch, Life of Phocion 17; the quote is from Homer, *Odyssey* 9.494.

11. Diodorus, *Library of History* 17.9.5.

12. Plutarch, Life of Phocion 17; Diodorus, *Library of History* 17.15.2.

13. Plutarch, Life of Phocion 18.

CHAPTER 11. APPROACHING THE BEGINNING OF THE END

1. Plutarch, Life of Agesilaus 15.

2. Plutarch, Life of Phocion 21.

3. Plutarch, Life of Phocion 21.

4. Aeschines, *Oration* 3.132–134.

5. Hyperides, Orations 5.31 ("Against Demosthenes").

6. Plutarch, Life of Phocion 22.

7. Plutarch, Life of Phocion 23.

8. Hippocrates, *Epidemics* 7.3, 4, 45; Plutarch, Life of Demosthenes 27.

9. Hyperides, Orations 6.13 ("Funeral Speech").

CHAPTER 12. CONFRONTING DISASTER AND REVENGE

1. Plutarch, Life of Phocion 26.

2. Plutarch, Life of Phocion 26.

3. Plutarch, Life of Phocion 27.

4. Plutarch, Life of Phocion 28; see also Martin and Sun, "'The Gods Were Supervising the Hardest-to-Handle Sufferings of Greece.'"

5. See, among others, Habicht, *Athens from Alexander to Antony*, 40–42; Mossé, *Athens in Decline*, 99–101; Romm, *Ghost on the Throne*, 128–131; Tritle, *Phocion the Good*, 129–137; Waterfield, *Dividing the Spoils*, 40–41.

6. Plutarch, Life of Phocion 30.

7. Plutarch, Life of Phocion 33.

8. Plutarch, Life of Phocion 34.

9. Plutarch, Life of Phocion 36.

10. Plutarch, Life of Phocion 37.

CHAPTER 13. THE MEMORY OF PHOCION, THEN, LATER, NOW

1. Hyperides, Orations 4.37 ("In Defense of Euxenippus").

2. Plutarch, Life of Phocion 4.

3. Plutarch, "Rules for Politicians," *Moralia* 823a.

4. Smith, *Theory of Moral Sentiments*, part 1, sect. 1, chap. 1: Of Sympathy.

Bibliography

ANCIENT SOURCES

Aelian. *Historical Miscellany.* Trans. N. G. Wilson. Loeb Classical Library 486. Cambridge: Harvard University Press, 1997.

Aeschines. *Aeschines.* Trans. Chris Carey. Austin: University of Texas Press, 2000.

Aristotle. *The Complete Works of Aristotle. The Revised Oxford Translation.* Ed. Jonathan Barnes. 2 vols. Princeton: Princeton University Press, 1984.

Cornelius Nepos. *The Book on the Great Generals of Foreign Nations.* Trans. J. C. Rolfe. Loeb Classical Library 467. Cambridge: Harvard University Press, 1929, 1984.

Demosthenes. *Demosthenes I: Orations 1–17 and 20. Olynthiacs, Philippics, Minor Public Speeches, Speech Against Leptines.* Trans. J. H. Vince. Loeb Classical Library 238. Cambridge: Harvard University Press, 1930.

———. *Demosthenes II: Orations 18–19. De Corona, De Falsa Legatione.* Trans. C. A. Vince and J. H. Vince. Loeb Classical Library 155 (Cambridge: Harvard University Press, 1939).

———. *Demosthenes VI. Orations 50–59. Private Cases, In Neaeram.* Trans. A. T. Murray. Loeb Classical Library 351. Cambridge: Harvard University Press, 1939.

Diodorus of Sicily. *The Library, Books 16–20. Philip II, Alexander the Great, and the Successors.* Trans. Robin Waterfield. Oxford: Oxford University Press, 2019.

Diogenes Laertius. *Lives of Eminent Philosophers.* Trans. R. D. Hicks. 2 vols. Loeb Classical Library 184–185. Cambridge: Harvard University Press, 1972.

Euripides. *Euripides: Four Plays. Medea, Hippolytus, Heracles, Bacchae.* Trans. Stephen Esposito. Newburyport, Mass.: Focus, 2004.

Harding, Phillip. *From the End of the Peloponnesian War to the Battle of Ipsus.* Vol. 2 in *Translated Documents of Greece and Rome,* ed. E. Badian and Robert K. Sherk. Cambridge: Cambridge University Press, 1985.

Hippocrates. *Hippocrates VII. Epidemics 2 and 4–7.* Trans. Wesley D. Smith. Loeb Classical Library 477. Cambridge: Harvard University Press, 1994.

Homer. *The Odyssey.* Trans. A. T. Murray. 2 vols. Loeb Classical Library 104–105. Cambridge: Harvard University Press, 1919.

Bibliography

Hyperides. Orations. In *Minor Attic Orators II. Lycurgus, Dinarchus, Demades, Hyperides.* Trans. J. O. Burtt. Loeb Classical Library 395. Cambridge: Harvard University Press, 1954.

Isaeus. *Orations.* Trans. E. S. Forster. Loeb Classical Library 202. Cambridge: Harvard University Press, 1927.

Isocrates. *Isocrates.* Trans. Terry L. Papillon. Austin: University of Texas Press, 2004.

Lycurgus. "Against Leocrites." In *Minor Attic Orators II. Lycurgus, Dinarchus, Demades, Hyperides.* Trans. J. O. Burtt. Loeb Classical Library 395. Cambridge: Harvard University Press, 1954.

Lysias. *Lysias.* Trans. W. R. M. Lamb. Loeb Classical Library 244. Cambridge: Harvard University Press, 1930.

Plato. *The Collected Dialogues Including the Letters.* Ed. Edith Hamilton and Huntington Cairns. Princeton: Princeton University Press, 1961.

Plutarch. Life of Agesilaus. In *Greek Lives.* Trans. Robin Waterfield. Oxford: Oxford University Press, 1998.

———. Life of Demosthenes. In *Hellenistic Lives. Including Alexander the Great.* Trans. Robin Waterfield. Oxford: Oxford University Press, 2016.

———. Life of Phocion. In *Hellenistic Lives. Including Alexander the Great.* Trans. Robin Waterfield. Oxford: Oxford University Press, 2016.

———. "Rules for Politicians," *Moralia* 798–825. In *Selected Essays and Dialogues.* Trans. Donald Russell. Oxford: Oxford University Press, 1993.

Valerius Maximus. *Memorable Doings and Sayings.* 2 vols. Ed. and trans. D. R. Shackleton Bailey. Loeb Classical Library 492–493. Cambridge: Harvard University Press, 2000.

Xenophon. *The Landmark Xenophon's "Hellenika."* Trans. John Marincola, ed. Robert B. Strassler. New York: Anchor, 2009.

MODERN SOURCES

Amyot, Jean-Jacques. *Les Vies des hommes illustres des Grecs et Romains, comparées l'une avec l'autre par Plutarque de Chaeronée.* Paris: Michel de Vascosan, 1559.

Bayliss, Andrew J. *After Demosthenes: The Politics of Early Hellenistic Athens.* London: Bloomsbury, 2011.

Bearzot, Cinzia. *Focione tra storia e trasfigurazione ideale.* Milan: Vite e Pensiero, 1985.

Beaumont, Lesley A. *Childhood in Ancient Athens: Iconography and Social History.* London: Routledge, 2012.

Bibliography

Bernays, Jacob. *Phokion und seine neueren Beurtheiler. Ein Beitrag zur Geschichte der griechischen Philosophie und Politik.* Berlin: Wilhelm Heltz, 1881.

Canevaro, Mirko. "Memory, the Orators, and the Public in Fourth-Century Athens." In *Greek Memories: Theory and Practice,* ed. Luca Castagnoli and Paola Ceccarelli, 136–157. Cambridge: Cambridge University Press, 2019.

Carter, L. B. *The Quiet Athenian.* Oxford: Clarendon, 1986.

Christ, Matthew. *The Bad Citizen in Classical Athens.* Cambridge: Cambridge University Press, 2006.

Duff, Timothy. *Plutarch's Lives. Exploring Virtue and Vice.* Oxford: Clarendon, 1999.

Erskine, Andrew. "Standing Up to the Demos: Plutarch, Phocion, and the Democratic Life." In *The Hellenistic Reception of Classical Athenian Democracy and Political Thought,* ed. Mirko Canevaro and Ben Gray, 237–259. Oxford: Oxford University Press, 2018.

Gabrielsen, Vincent. *Financing the Athenian Fleet: Public Taxation and Social Relations.* Baltimore: Johns Hopkins University Press, 1994.

——. "The Navies of Classical Athens and Hellenistic Rhodes: An Epigraphic Comparison." *Revue des études militaires anciennes* 6 (2013): 63–79.

Garber, Marjorie. "Good to Think With." In Garber, *Loaded Words,* 94–103. New York: Fordham University Press, 2012.

Garland, Robert. *Daily Life of the Ancient Greeks.* Westport, Conn.: Greenwood, 1998.

Gehrke, Hans-Joachim. *Phokion. Studien zur Erfassung seiner historischen Gestalt.* Munich: C. H. Beck, 1976.

Geiger, Joseph. "Death of a Statesman: Poussin's Phocion." In *The Statesman in Plutarch's Works.* Vol. 1: *Plutarch's Statesman and His Aftermath: Political, Philosophical, and Literary Aspects,* ed. Jeroen Bons et al., 287–296. Leiden: Brill, 2004.

Golden, Mark. *Children and Childhood in Classical Athens.* 2nd ed. Baltimore: Johns Hopkins University Press, 2015.

Habicht, Christian. *Athens from Alexander to Antony.* Trans. Deborah Lucas Schneider. Cambridge: Harvard University Press, 1997.

Hamilton, Alexander. *A Letter from Phocion to the Considerate Citizens of New York, on the Politics of the Day.* New York: Samuel Loudon, 1784.

——. *A Second Letter from Phocion to the Considerate Citizens of New York, on the Politics of the Day.* New York: Samuel Loudon, 1784.

Hansen, Mogens Herman. *The Athenian Democracy in the Age of Demosthenes: Structure, Principles and Ideology.* 2nd ed. Trans. J. A. Crook. Oxford: Blackwell, 1999.

Bibliography

Hanson, Victor Davis, ed. *Hoplites: The Classical Greek Battle Experience*. London: Routledge, 1991.

Harding, Phillip E. *Athens Transformed, 404–262 BC: From Popular Sovereignty to the
Dominion of Wealth*. New York: Routledge, 2015.

Herman, Gabriel. *Morality and Behaviour in Democratic Athens*. Cambridge: Cambridge
University Press, 2006.

Jacobs, Susan G. *Plutarch's Pragmatic Biographies: Lessons for Statesmen and Generals in
the "Parallel Lives."* Leiden: Brill, 2017.

Kamen, Deborah. *Insults in Classical Athens*. Madison: University of Wisconsin Press,
2020.

Lamont, Jessica L. "Athenian Curse Practice." In *In Blood and Ashes: Curse Tablets and
Binding Spells in Ancient Greece,* ed. Jessica L Lamont, 134–188. Oxford: Oxford
University Press, 2023.

Lévi-Strauss, Claude. *Le Totémisme aujourd'hui*. Paris: Presses Universitaires de France,
1962.

Mably, Gabriel Bonnet de. *Entretiens de Phocion, sur le rapport de la morale avec la poli-
tique*. Zurich: Heidegguer, 1763.

Martin, Thomas R. *Ancient Greece: From Prehistoric to Hellenistic Times*. 2nd ed. New
Haven: Yale University Press, 2013.

Martin, Thomas R., and Christopher W. Blackwell. *Alexander the Great: The Story of
an Ancient Life*. Cambridge: Cambridge University Press, 2012.

Martin, Thomas R., and Ivy Sui-yuen Sun. "'The Gods Were Supervising the Hardest-
to-Handle Sufferings of Greece': The Meaning of *Episkopein* in Plutarch, *Phocion*
28." *Rationes Rerum* 9 (2017): 93–112.

Morrison, J. S., J. F. Coates, and N. B. Rankov. *The Athenian Trireme: The History and
Reconstruction of an Ancient Greek Warship*. 2nd ed. Cambridge: Cambridge University Press, 2000.

Mossé, Claude. *Athens in Decline, 404–86 B.C.* Trans. Jean Stewart. London: Routledge
and Kegan Paul, 1973.

Neils, Jenifer, and Dylan K. Rogers, eds. *The Cambridge Companion to Ancient Athens*.
Cambridge: Cambridge University Press, 2021.

North, Thomas. *The Lives of the Noble Grecians and Romanes Compared Together by That
Grave Learned Philosopher and Historiographer, Plutarke of Chaeronea*. London:
Richard Field, 1579.

Ober, Josiah. *Political Dissent in Democratic Athens: Intellectual Critics of Popular Rule*.
Princeton: Princeton University Press, 1998.

Bibliography

Oliver, Graham J. *War, Food, and Politics in Early Hellenistic Athens.* Oxford: Oxford University Press, 2007.

Pritchard, David M. *Athenian Democracy at War.* Cambridge: Cambridge University Press, 2019.

Rhodes, P. J., and Robin Osborne. *Greek Historical Inscriptions, 404–323 BC.* Oxford: Oxford University Press, 2003.

Richard, Carl J. "Plutarch and the Early American Republic." In *A Companion to Plutarch,* ed. Mark Beck, 598–610. Malden, Mass.: Wiley Blackwell, 2013.

Romm, James. *Ghost on the Throne: The Death of Alexander the Great and the War for Crown and Empire.* New York: Knopf, 2011.

Schwenk, Cynthia. "Athens." In *The Greek World in the Fourth Century: From the Fall of the Athenian Empire to the Successors of Alexander the Great,* ed. Lawrence C. Tritle, 8–40. London: Routledge, 1997.

Sealey, Raphael. *Demosthenes and His Time: A Study in Defeat.* New York: Oxford University Press, 1993.

Simmons, Robert Holschuh. *Demagogues, Power, and Friendship in Classical Athens.* London: Bloomsbury, 2023.

Smith, Adam. *The Theory of Moral Sentiments.* 2nd ed. Edinburgh: A. Millar, A. Kinkaid, and J. Bell, 1761.

Smith, William Laughton. *The Pretensions of Thomas Jefferson to the Presidency Examined; and the Charges Against John Adams Refuted. Addressed to the Citizens of America in General; and Particularly to the Electors of the President.* 2 vols. Philadelphia: Fenno, 1796.

Steefel, Lawrence D., Jr. "A Narrative Reading of Poussin's *Phocion* Paintings." *Kunsthistorisk tidskrift/Journal of Art History* 60 (1991): 9–16.

Tajfel, Henri, and John C. Turner. "The Social Identity Theory of Intergroup Behavior." In *Political Psychology: Key Readings,* ed. John T. Jost and Jim Sidanius, 276–293. New York: Psychology Press, 2004.

Thérive, André (Candidus d'Isaurie). *Vie de Phocion.* Paris: Clé d'Or, 1948.

Tritle, Lawrence A. *Phocion the Good.* London: Croom Helm, 1988.

——. "Forty-Five or What? The Generalships of Phocion." *Liverpool Classical Monthly* 17 (1992): 19–23.

Tritle, Lawrence A., ed. *The Greek World in the Fourth Century: From the Fall of the Athenian Empire to the Successors of Alexander.* London: Routledge, 1997.

Waterfield, Robin. *Dividing the Spoils: The War for Alexander the Great's Empire.* Oxford: Oxford University Press, 2012.

Acknowledgments

I would like to thank James Romm, series editor, for the invitation to contribute to the Ancient Lives series; the three anonymous scholars who reviewed the manuscript for Yale University Press for their perceptive and direct comments and corrections; Thomas Herbertson for his expert proofreading and suggestions for revision of an early draft; Susan Laity of Yale University Press for her superb editing of the final version; and Heather Gold and Elizabeth Sylvia of Yale University Press for their invaluable support throughout.

Special thanks go to Megan Edwards for her insight and encouragement as an author who successfully links the history of the past with the truths of fiction to create compelling narratives.

Index

Academos, 66

Aeschines, 32; as defendant against Demosthenes, 131–132; and feud with Demosthenes, 153–154

Aeschylus, *Agamemnon*, 78

Agamemnon, 78–79, 139

Agesilaus (Spartan king), 78–80, 83, 84, 86, 111

agora (Athens), 33

Alcetus (king of Epirus), 104

Alexander (son of Polyperchon), 174–175

Alexander the Great, 1, 7, 37, 120; as admirer of Phocion, 146–147; death of, 157–158; and demand that Greeks recognize him as a god, 155–156; early successes of, 143–145; as king of Macedonia, 142; Phocion's concerns regarding, 143, 144–147; Theban rebellion against, 144

Amphiaraus, oracle of, 107

Amphipolis, Philip's capture of, 124

Amphis, 67

Amyntas (king of Macedonia), 104

Amyot, Jean-Jacques, as translator of Plutarch's *Parallel Lives*, 184

Anniceris, 69

Antigonus One-Eye, 170, 181, 182

Antipater: after Alexander's death, 158; as Alexander's deputy, 149–150, 151; Greeks at war with, 158–161; harsh punishments imposed by, 163–165; Phocion as commander against, 159; and Phocion's efforts on behalf of the Athenians, 166–167; Phocion's meeting with, 163–164; Phocion's relationship with, 168–169; scholarly debate surrounding Antipater's impact on Athenian society, 167, 188; Successors and, 170, 181; as threat to Athens, 158–161, 163–164

Apollo at Delphi, oracle of, 129, 135

archons, 61–62; responsibilities of, 63

Aristotle, 31; on techniques of persuasion, 190–191

Artaxerxes II (Persian Great King), 78, 79, 81, 107; and the Satraps' Revolt, 110–111, 125; treaty negotiated by, 82

Artaxerxes III (Persian Great King), 117, 124

Asclepius, 29, 140

Assembly: challenges of speaking to, 57–58; as decision-making body for Athenian democracy, 56–58; Phocion's address to, regarding Oropos, 107–108; stipend paid for attendance at, 56

Athena, festival honoring, 114

Athenian courts: *dikasteria*'s role in, 60–61; jurors' role in, 60–61

Athenian democracy, 1–2, 11; age requirement for participation in, 62–63; Assembly's role in, 56–58, 59–60; Council of Five Hundred's role in, 58–60; Council of the Areopagus's role in, 61–62, 156; courts' role in, 60–61; as divided

Index

Athenian democracy (*continued*)
democracy, 99; generals' role in,
63–65; participants in, 62–64;
Phocion's concerns regarding, 156;
Phocion's role in, 1–2; structure of,
55–56
Athenian men: competition among,
26–27, 28; corporal punishment
doled out to, 26–27; expectations
of, 25–26, 33; initiations experienced by, 41; military service required of, 43–45; sexual relationships among, 27–28; symposiums
as enjoyed by, 33–34
Athenian military: and alliance with
Spartans, 106–107; cavalrymen in,
51–52; commanders in, 50–51; expectations of, 51; generals' role in,
63–65; hoplites as part of, 45–50,
64; importance of, 43; infantry
as part of, 45–47, 52; navy as part
of, 52–54; Philip's demands of,
140–141; as requirement for adult
male citizens, 44–45; resources
required for, 54; and the Satraps'
Revolt, 110–111; slaves' role in,
47–48, 53; structure of, 45–54;
training required for, 43–44,
49–50, 52
Athenian naval power. *See* trierarchs;
triremes
Athenian society: accusations of corruption in, 156–157; adoption of adults
in, 19; and allegiance to Cassander,
182; athletic training in, 25–26;
autochthony as important to, 35–36,
37–39; autonomy in, 21–22; babies
at risk in, 15–16; "barbarians" as
viewed in, 36–37; childhood in,
13–14, 29; citizenship in, 37–39;
coming-of-age ceremony in, 39–40;
competition as aspect of, 26–27, 28;
early training in civic and religious
values in, 28–29; education in,
22–24; father-son relationships in,
30–32; festivals celebrated by, 29;
fragility of life in, 18–20; lack of
sanitation in, 18; military service
in, 22–23, 25–26, 33, 43–46; money
and class as factor in, 14–15, 17–18,
22–24; parent-child relationships
in, 31–32; pedagogues in, 23–24,
31; Phocion as critic of, 4–5, 8–9;
political divisions within, 8; poverty
in, 18; religious rituals as important
to, 29; risks and dangers inherent
in, 15–20; sense of belonging as
important to, 3–4, 21, 36, 38–41,
152; slaves in, 20–21; Spartans'
punitive treatment of, 76–87; and
tensions with Alexander, 155; uncertainty as constant in, 16–17;
women in, 14, 20–21, 38
Athenian women, 14, 20–21, 38; laws
affecting, 150; and risks of childbirth, 16–17, 19
Athens: administrative government of,
40–41, 99–100; Alexander as threat
to, 143–146; and alliances with
other Greek city-states, 79–80,
106–107, 109; Antipater as threat
to, 158–161, 163–164; citizenship
as achieved in, 37–40; coming-of-
age ceremony in, 39; construction
projects in, 150; debate over the
meaning of democracy in, 118–119;
end of democracy in, 1–2, 11; expectations of officials in, 104–105;
history of, 69–71; and the King's
Peace, 81, 103; and the Lamian
War, 159–161; Long Walls of, 76;
under Lycurgus, 150–151; musical
performances in, 28, 29; and ongoing hostilities with the Spartans,

Index

103–104; Persians as allies of, 79–80; Persians as threat to, 37, 76–77, 110–112; political environment of, upon Phocion's coming-of-age, 76–78; population of, 39; under Roman control, 183; size of, 39; Spartans' victory over, 69–71, 100; Thebans as threat to, 106–107, 109–110. *See also* Second Athenian League

Attica. *See* Athens

"barbarians," 36–37
Bearzot, Cinzia, 188
belonging, sense of: as important for political leadership, 190–193; as important to Athenians, 3–4, 21, 36, 38–41, 152
Bernays, Jacob, 187
Boeotians, and hostilities with the Spartans, 79
Bosporus Strait, 118
Byzantium, 118; Macedonian aggression against, 134, 135

Caesar, Julius, 3
Callistratus, charged with treason over Oropos, 108
Candidus of Isauria (André Thérive), 187–188
Cassander, 181, 182; as rival of Polyperchon, 170–171, 172, 175
Cato, Marcus Porcius, 3, 185
Chabrias, 67, 101; charged with treason, 108; death of, 119; as influence on Phocion, 83, 103; as military leader, 83–85, 86–87, 89, 95–96, 105; Phocion as influence on, 95–96, 100–101; and the Satraps' Revolt, 111
Chaeronea, Battle of, 135–137; aftermath of, 137–141

Chares, 119; as controversial figure, 134
Charidemus, 137–138, 145
childbirth, risks of, 16–17
childhood experiences, impact of, on adult perspective, 13–16, 21–24
citizenship process in Athens, 37–39
Clearchus, 173
Cleombrotus I (Spartan king), 83, 106
Conon (naval commander), 80, 173
Corcyra, Spartans in control of, 140
Corinth, League of, 140–141, 142, 151; following Philip's death, 143; rebellion against, 158
Corinthian War, 79–81
corporal punishment as common practice, 26–27
Council of Five Hundred, 33, 40, 58–60, 81, 100, 143, 151
Council of the Areopagus, 61–62, 138, 156
curses, significance of, in ancient Greece, 57, 116
Cyprus, 125
Cyrus (brother of Artaxerxes II), 78

Darius I (Persian Great King), 77
Darius III (Persian Great King), 149
Deinarchus, 176
Delian League, 85–86, 95
Demades, 138–139, 140, 146, 157, 166
demes, 40–41
Demeter, 101, 165
Demetrius of Phaleron, as governor of Athens, 182, 183
Demetrius the Besieger, 182
democracy and democracies: Hamilton's concerns regarding, 2, 186; Phocion cited in arguments concerning, 185–187. *See also* Athenian democracy
Demosthenes, 54, 93, 97, 108, 126, 144, 145, 152; on Alexander's proposal to

Index

Demosthenes (*continued*)
    be recognized as a god, 156; and
    efforts to resist Philip II, 122, 127,
    129–130, 134, 136; as famed orator,
    32, 137; and feud with Aeschines,
    153–154; and the Lamian War, 160;
    on news of Philip's assassination,
    143; prosecuted for corruption,
    155–156; as prosecutor against
    Aeschines, 131–132; sentenced to
    death by Antipater, 166; and the
    war against Antipater, 160
Dercyllus, 173
dikasteria (institutions for determining
    justice), 60–61
Dionysius I (ruler of Sicily), 69
Dionysus (divinity), 155
Diotimus, 97

Epaminondas, 109–110
Ephebic Oath, 43–44
Eretria, Phocion as defender of, 133.
    See also Plutarch of Eretria, and
    the dispute over Euboea
Euboea: Athenians' loss of, 127; as
    member of the Second Athenian
    League, 120; Phocion's involvement
    in dispute over, 125–127
Euripides, *Medea*, 16–17
Exiles Decree, issued by Alexander, 155
exposure of unwanted babies, 16

Faulkner, William, *Requiem for a Nun*, 12

Gehrke, Jans-Joachim, 188
Great Mysteries (sacred ritual), 101
Greek city-states: and alliances between
    Athens and other city-states,
    79–80, 106–107, 109; after the
    Battle of Chaeronea, 141–142;
    Philip's dominance over, 140–142

Hagnonides, 166–167, 175–176, 177
Hamilton, Alexander, "Phocion" as
    pseudonym used by, 2, 186
Harpalus, thief of Alexander's treasury,
    154–155, 156, 157
Hellespont, as crucial for Athenians,
    81–82
Heracles, 36, 155
Hesiod, 155
Hippocrates, 160
Homer: *Iliad*, 78, 138–139; *Odyssey*, 144
hoplites, 45–48, 49, 64; armor worn by,
    46–47, 160
Hyperides, 131, 137, 157, 189; sentenced
    to death by Antipater, 166

Idomeneus, 14
infection, risks associated with, 18
Iphicrates, 47, 81, 92, 119
Iphigenia, 78
Isaeus, 19
Isocrates, 82–83, 106, 118; and advice
    to Athenians, 124; *Areopagiticus*,
    118
isonomia (equality in citizenship), and
    Athenian democracy, 56, 119

Jason (ruler of Pherae), 104
Jefferson, Thomas, 186–187

King's Peace, terms of, 82, 103, 105
koureion (coming-of-age ceremony), 39

Lamian War, 159–160
Leon, 135
Leonnatus, 160
Leos (son of Orpheus), 40–41
Leosthenes, 158, 160
Leuctra, Battle of, 106, 108
Lévi-Strauss, Claude, 10–11
Lycidas, 81

Index

Lycurgus, 137; legislation proposed by, 150–151

Lysias, 97

Lysicles, 137

Mably, Gabriel Bonnet de, *Entretiens de Phocion*, 185–186

Macedonia: army of, 123; leadership structure of, 121–122; people of, 120–121; Philip II as military leader of, 122–130, 133–135; turmoil in, following Philip's assassination, 142–143. *See also* Alexander the Great; Philip II

Makartatos, 97–98

Mantinea, Battle of, 109–110, 120

Mausolus, 117

Megara, Athenian support for, 130

Menyllus, 168–171

military service: and Athenian warfare, 49–51, 52–54; outfitting of troops, 45–48; payment of military, 51–54; as required of Athenian men, 43–45, 48

Naxos, Battle of, 89, 135; Phocion as hero of, 94–95, 101

Nepos, Cornelius, 14

Nicanor, 170–174, 175–76, 189

North, Sir Thomas, *The Lives of the Noble Grecians and Romanes Compared*, 184

Odevaere, Joseph Denis, painting of Phocion's death scene, 185

Olympias (Alexander the Great's mother), 172, 174

Olynthus, Philip's capture of, 128–129

Oropos: aftermath of battle of, 110; battle for control over, 107–108; Phocion's involvement with, 107–108

Orpheus, 41

Panathenaic festival, 114

pankration (sport), 26

Peloponnesian War, 69–70

Perdiccas (king of Macedonia), 122

Pericles, 34, 37, 64, 138

Perinthus, Macedonian aggression against, 134

Persephone, 101

Persian Empire: Alexander's campaign against, 147; Athenian alliance with, 79–80; as threat to Athenians, 37, 76–77, 110–112. *See also individual Great Kings*

Philip II (king of Macedonia), 7, 120; assassination of, 142; Athenians at war with, 134–135; and the Battle of Chaeronea, 135–137, 139; and dispute over Euboea, 125–126; and dispute over Olynthus, 128–129; as king, 122–123; as military leader, 122–130; Phocion in opposition to, 133–134, 139; tactical innovations developed by, 123; at Thermopylae, 129

Philip III Arrhidaeus (king of Macedonia), 142, 158, 170, 176–177

Philocrates, peace agreement negotiated by, 128–129, 131

Phocion: advice of, following the Battle of Chaeronea, 138–139, 140, 141; Alexander as admirer of, 146–147; on Alexander's death, 158; as antagonistic toward some segments of Athenian society, 41–42; and Antipater's terms of surrender, 163–165; assessments of, 10, 190–193; as Athenian statesman, 1, 41–42; and betrayal by Nicanor, 173; Chabrias as influence on, 83, 193; as citizen of Athens, 35, 38; as commander of a warship, 86–87;

Index

Phocion (*continued*)
and concerns about war against
Antipater, 158–159; cremation and
burial of, 179–180; curse tablets
directed at, 116; as defender against
Macedonian aggression, 133–135;
denounced as traitor, 1–2, 7,
175–179; as different from his
contemporaries, 113–14; early
biographies of, 185–190; education
of, 14, 22, 23–24, 30, 65–68, 72–73;
and the end of Athenian democracy,
1–2, 11–12, 181–183; elected to serve
as general, 1, 64, 123, 124, 125, 151;
elite family status of, 4, 14–15, 48,
54; and emotional connections as
important for political leaders,
190–191; execution of, 9, 179;
family of, 103; financial circumstances of, 14–15, 112–116; generosity of, 114; as harsh critic of
Athenian society, 4–5, 8–9; honored as Chrestos, 7, 114; hostility
toward, 116; as influence on
Chabrias, 95–96, 100–101; last
moments of, 178–179; last years of,
167–169; as member of Leontis
tribe, 40–41; as mercenary for a
Persian monarch, 124–125; as military leader, 41, 44, 45, 50–51, 54,
64, 86–87, 89–97, 101, 103, 105,
133–135; military service of, 6–7,
48–51; as naval commander, 54,
89–97, 101; on news of Philip's
assassination, 143; perceived as
conspiring with Nicanor, 171–173;
Plato as influence on, 72–73, 85; at
Plato's Academy, 30, 66–68, 72–73;
Plutarch on, 3, 4–5, 14, 101, 184,
185–186; as political leader, 7, 136,
139, 144–145; principles influencing
his decisions, 66; public conduct of,

34–35, 95–96; public service career
of, 75–76; and Pythias, 152; questions regarding truthfulness of,
115–116; reasons for failure of,
192–193; and relationship with his
son, 32; and relevance to our own
times, 2, 10–12, 152, 191–193; and
reluctance to socialize with other
men, 33–35, 192; as represented in
art, 185; revised reputation of, 183;
safety as preoccupation of, 5–6,
7–8, 17–20, 72–73, 75, 80, 109,
133, 152; and the Satraps' Revolt,
111–112; scholarly debate over
reputation of, 181; sentenced to
death, 177–179; sources for background on, 2–3; as *strategos*, 102,
123, 124, 130, 151; and support for
the Megarians, 130; as trierarch, 54,
89–97; as viewed by early modern
commentators, 9–10, 185–188; as
witness in trial involving Demosthenes and Aeschines, 130–132. *See
also* Athenian men
Phocion (Phocion's grandfather), 15
Phocus (Phocion's son), 14, 178; education of, 113–114; self-indulgent
lifestyle of, 114
phratry (fraternal society), 39
Plataea, Thebans' attack on, 105–106
Plato, 13, 14, 17; background of, 69; on
the Good in politics, 68–69; as
influence on Phocion, 72–73, 85;
Republic, 72; as speaker on behalf
of Callistratus, 108
Plato's Academy, 14, 66–68; dialogues
as focus of, 67–68; Phocion as
student at, 30, 66–68
Plutarch (biographer), 6; biographies as
inspiration for artists, 185; *Parallel
Lives*, 2–3; on Phocion, 3, 14, 101,
127; on Phocion's rhetoric, 4–5; on

Index

Phocion's son, 113; popularity of
biographies by, 184–186
Plutarch of Eretria, and the dispute over
Euboea, 126–127
political leadership, desirable attributes
for, 190–193
Polyperchon, as successor to Antipater,
170, 171–174, 176–177, 181, 182
Poussin, Nicolas, paintings based on
Phocion's fate, 185
Pytheas: and the Lamian War, 160; and
Phocion, 152

religious rituals, in ancient Athens, 29,
101
Roxane (wife of Alexander the Great),
158

Salamis, Battle of, 165
Satraps' Revolt, 110–111, 125
Second Athenian League, 85–86, 95;
Byzantium's withdrawal from, 118;
divisions within, 118–120; Euboea
as member of, 120; financial strains
experienced by, 117–118; setbacks
experienced by, 120–124
slaves, in the Athenian military, 47–48, 53
Smith, Adam, *Theory of Moral Sentiments*, 193
Smith, William Loughton: "Phocion"
as pseudonym used by, 186–187
Social War, 118
Socrates, 67, 70, 112, 179, 185; as
depicted by Jacques-Louis David,
185; trial of, 30, 71–72
Solon, 61
Sparta and Spartans, 35–36; Athenian
alliance with, 106–107, 109;
Athenians' defeat by, 69–71, 100;
after the Battle of Chaeronea,
139–140; and ongoing hostilities
with the Athenians, 103–104;

Persian support sought by, 81; and
punitive treatment of Athenians,
76–87; and rebellion against Macedonian rule, 149; Thebans as threat
to, 106–107, 109; at war with the
Persians, 78–79
strategos (general): Phocion as, 102, 123,
124, 130, 151; role of in Athenian
democracy, 64–65
symposiums, 33–34

Thebans, 35; and attack on Plataea,
105–106
Thebes: Alexander as threat to, 144–145;
Athenian alliance with, 85; after the
Battle of Chaeronea, 139–140;
Spartans' attack on, 106
Thérive, André, *Vie de Phocion*, 187–188
Thermopylae, Philip's march through, 129
Thessalians, Athenian alliance with, 120
Thessaly, Philip II as archon of, 129
Third Sacred War, 129
Thirty Tyrants, 70–71, 76, 79
Thucydides, 138
Timotheus, 90–91, 104–105, 119
totemism, 11
trierarchs: abuses of power by, 97–99;
logistical challenges faced by, 92–93;
obligations and responsibilities of,
89–95; Phocion as, 54, 89–97
triremes, 52–53; commanders of, 54,
89–90; crew members needed for,
91–92, 93; dangers to rowers of,
91–92, 93; private misuses of,
97–98. *See also* trierarchs
Tritle, Lawrence A., *Phocion the Good*,
188–189
Trojan War, 78

Xenocrates of Chalcedon, 72, 164, 168
Xenophon, 71, 76, 110
Xerxes (Persian Great King), 77